Marketo Mastery: Proven Tips for a Successful Implementation

Ethan A. Cox

All rights reserved. Copyright © 2023 Ethan A. Cox

COPYRIGHT © 2023 Ethan A. Cox

All rights reserved.

No part of this book must be reproduced, stored in a retrieval system, or shared by any means, electronic, mechanical, photocopying, recording, or otherwise, without written permission from the publisher.

Every precaution has been taken in the preparation of this book; still the publisher and author assume no responsibility for errors or omissions. Nor do they assume any liability for damages resulting from the use of the information contained herein.

Legal Notice:

This book is copyright protected and is only meant for your individual use. You are not allowed to amend, distribute, sell, use, quote or paraphrase any of its part without the written consent of the author or publisher.

Introduction

Embarking on a journey through the intricate world of Marketo, we unravel the secrets to effective program implementation—unlocking its power, precision, and strategic brilliance.

Organizational finesse emerges as a cornerstone, as we delve into the art of foldering and naming conventions. The operational folder orchestrates your command center, while the archive folder preserves your historical assets. Meanwhile, the design studio becomes your creative haven, while the database empowers your marketing pursuits.

Strategic insights await in the realm of analytics, while the program naming convention becomes your guiding star. This strategic framework infuses clarity, consistency, and synergy, paving the way for an organized Marketo landscape.

In the realm of execution, a well-crafted smart-campaign naming convention is your ally. This blueprint streamlines campaign management, ensuring logic and coherence in the midst of complexity.

The journey further extends to asset naming convention, where coherence reigns. Discover a naming strategy that fosters familiarity and productivity, aligning your assets in harmonious symphony.

Operational programs and data management elevate your Marketo experience. Traverse the nuances of data orchestration and process optimization, mastering the art of seamless operations.

The potency of nurture programs and strategy comes alive, enabling you to orchestrate value-driven campaigns that guide leads along the buyer's journey. Personalization and engagement take center stage.

Lead scoring best practices shine a light on quantifying lead readiness. Grasp the intricacies of scoring methodologies, bridging marketing and sales seamlessly.

In the world of PPC (Pay Per Click) programs, strategic advertising finds its voice. Crafting compelling ads and optimizing landing pages elevate your digital efforts to new heights.

This book guides you through each layer of Marketo's potential. As you craft campaigns, nurture sequences, and dive into data management, this guide stands as your trusted companion—a journey through strategic brilliance and operational excellence.

Contents

Chapter 1 - Foldering & NamingConventions..1
    Operational Folder..8
    Archive Folder..8
    Design Studio...9
    Database..13
    Analytics..18
    Program Naming Convention...20
    Smart-Campaign Naming Convention..23
    Asset Naming Convention..26
Chapter 2 - Operational Programs & DataManagement...30
    Flow Tab Criteria:..33
    Smart List Tab Criteria...38
    Flow Tab Criteria:..38
    Schedule Tab Criteria:..39
    Smart List Tab Criteria...40
    Flow Tab Criteria:..40
    Schedule Tab Criteria:..41
    Campaign 01 - Hard Bounce > Email InvalidSmart List Tab Criteria 42
    Flow Tab Criteria:..43
    Schedule Tab Criteria:..44
    Campaign 02 - Soft Bounce > Email Invalid 46
    Flow Tab Criteria:..47
    Schedule Tab Criteria:..48
    Campaign 03 - Reset Email InvalidSmart List Tab Criteria 50

- Flow Tab Criteria: 50
- Schedule Tab Criteria: 51
- Smart List Tab Criteria 54
- Flow Tab Criteria: 54
- Schedule Tab Criteria: 55
- Applying Dynamic Content in Assets 68
- Chapter 3 – Nurture Programs & Strategy 73
  - TOFU – NURTURE PROGRAM 75
  - Smart List Tab Criteria 76
  - Transition Rule Smart-List: 81
  - Smart List Tab Criteria 83
  - Flow Tab Criteria: 84
  - Smart List Tab Criteria 86
  - Flow Tab Criteria: 87
  - Smart List Tab Criteria 88
  - Flow Tab Criteria: 90
  - MOFU – NURTURE PROGRAM 93
  - Smart List Tab Criteria 94
  - Flow Tab Criteria: 95
  - Smart List Tab Criteria: 97
  - Flow Tab Criteria: 99
  - Smart List Tab Criteria: 100
  - Flow Tab Criteria: 101
  - Smart List Tab Criteria: 102
  - Flow Tab Criteria: 103
  - BOFU – NURTURE PROGRAM 104
  - Smart List Tab Criteria: 105

Flow Tab Criteria:	106
Smart List Tab Criteria:	108
Flow Tab Criteria:	109
Smart List Tab Criteria:	110
Flow Tab Criteria:	111
Customer Nurture	112
Opportunity-"Closed-Lost"-Reason-Captured Nurture	113
Other Types of Nurtures: Default-Program-TypeNurtures & Nested Programs	114
Chapter 4 – Lead Scoring Best Practices	123
Why Customize?	126
Should I score higher or lower?	126
How to calculate your MQL threshold?	127
Lead Scoring Program(s)	129
Step 1:	129
Behavioral Scoring	130
Smart List Tab Criteria:	131
Flow Tab Criteria:	131
Demographic Scoring	135
Smart List Tab Criteria:	136
Flow Tab Criteria:	136
Schedule Tab Criteria:	143
Chapter 5 – PPC (Pay Per Click) Programs	148
Once your Marketo Ad program is created:	158
Conclusion	160

Chapter 1 - Foldering & Naming Conventions

As with any investment in MarTech, you'll most likely want to start off with the right foot forward. Marketo is a large application and many organizations pay hefty sums to have someone walk them through proper implementation. That's why setting it up incorrectly from the start can be disastrous for future use. One of the first mistakes commonly seen in marketing-ops teams is the roll of the eyes when mentioning simple Marketo instance-organization. Many want to rush into the building campaigns and blasting off emails. They don't think about what may happen in 6 months if there is no thoughtful strategy behind how they'll name their marketing programs, smart-campaigns, or various assets. At best, most simply create folders with names that make sense to that person at the moment but won't for others who use the application later.

All too often, I've seen folks who don't put in this minor effort at the start of their implementation. They regret it later if it's pointed out to them, or worse when it comes time for reporting. This brings me to my point and the purpose of why I've chosen to start off with this topic. Considering your foldering and naming conventions will have benefits if you are just starting your implementation or even if you're inheriting a messy instance. If you are just implementing for the first time, your instance may look empty right now but imagine 6 months from now, or even 1 year. You may have hundreds of campaigns, programs, and even assets and it may be daunting to have to search, filter, and play detective to find what you need.

Or, if you're the lucky new owner of an inherited Marketo instance that may not be so clean, the same benefits apply to you. The problem in this scenario is the undertaking to improve the existing foldering and naming structure to something more scalable, and then strictly enforcing it with other Marketo admins' that also login, not to mention keeping up with your day-to-day tasks. But the benefits will be worthwhile in either case! Below are just a few reasons why we're diving into best practices for foldering and naming conventions:

- Quickly find exactly what you need

- Easily report on any marketing programs

- De-clutter & accelerate your pick-lists

- Keep your instance organized & pleasant to use

Let's start off with folders! The main purpose for folders is to organize your marketing programs, campaigns, and assets. But they also have some other interesting nuances related to them that everyone should be aware of. First, you won't be able to report on folders themselves. You may only report on what's within them such as the smart-campaign and asset metrics:

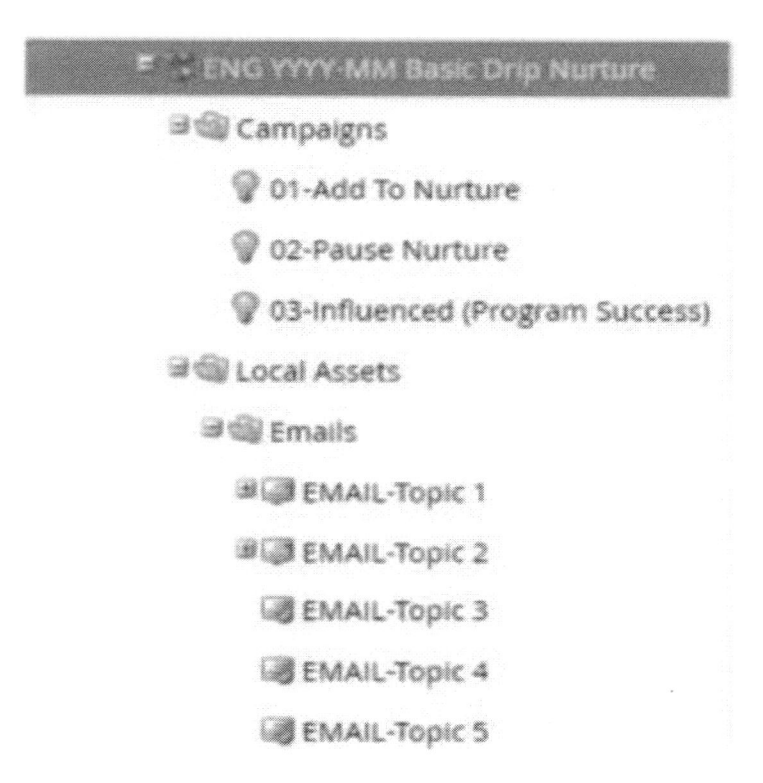

```
▼ ENG YYYY-MM Basic Drip Nurture
    ▣ Campaigns
        ♀ 01-Add To Nurture
        ♀ 02-Pause Nurture
        ♀ 03-Influenced (Program Success)
    ▣ Local Assets
        ▣ Emails
            ▣ EMAIL-Topic 1
            ▣ EMAIL-Topic 2
               EMAIL-Topic 3
               EMAIL-Topic 4
               EMAIL-Topic 5
```

Secondly, they sort alphanumerically, which we'll discuss how to use to our advantage later in this chapter. They also must have unique names when created under the same parent folder, or program. Otherwise, you'll get an error letting you know another folder with that name already exists.

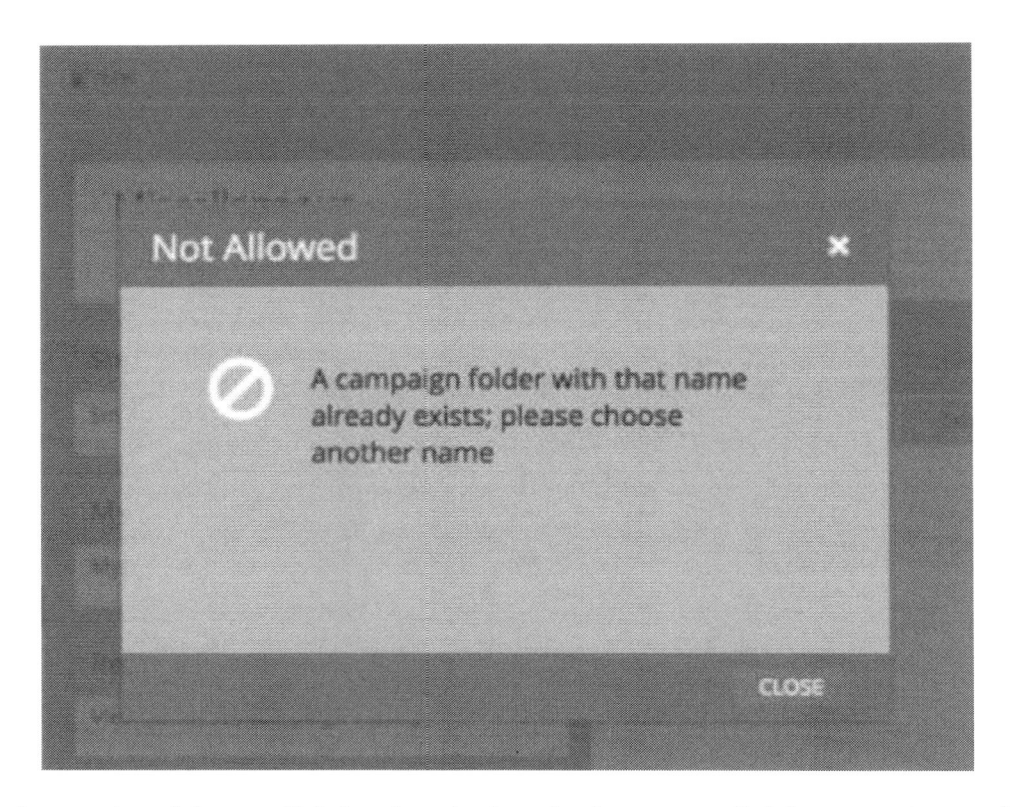

So how should you think about structuring your folders and creating a strategy around that? Glad you asked! There are four areas that we'll discuss and walkthrough when deciding what a good baseline for folders structures you should start off with. If you're inheriting an instance, you'll most likely need to work backward to untangle a labyrinth of random folders and put some sense to structuring them. The below suggestions should aid you in terms of thinking about how you should go about re-organizing your current foldering structure.

We'll start off with the Marketing Activities section in Marketo.

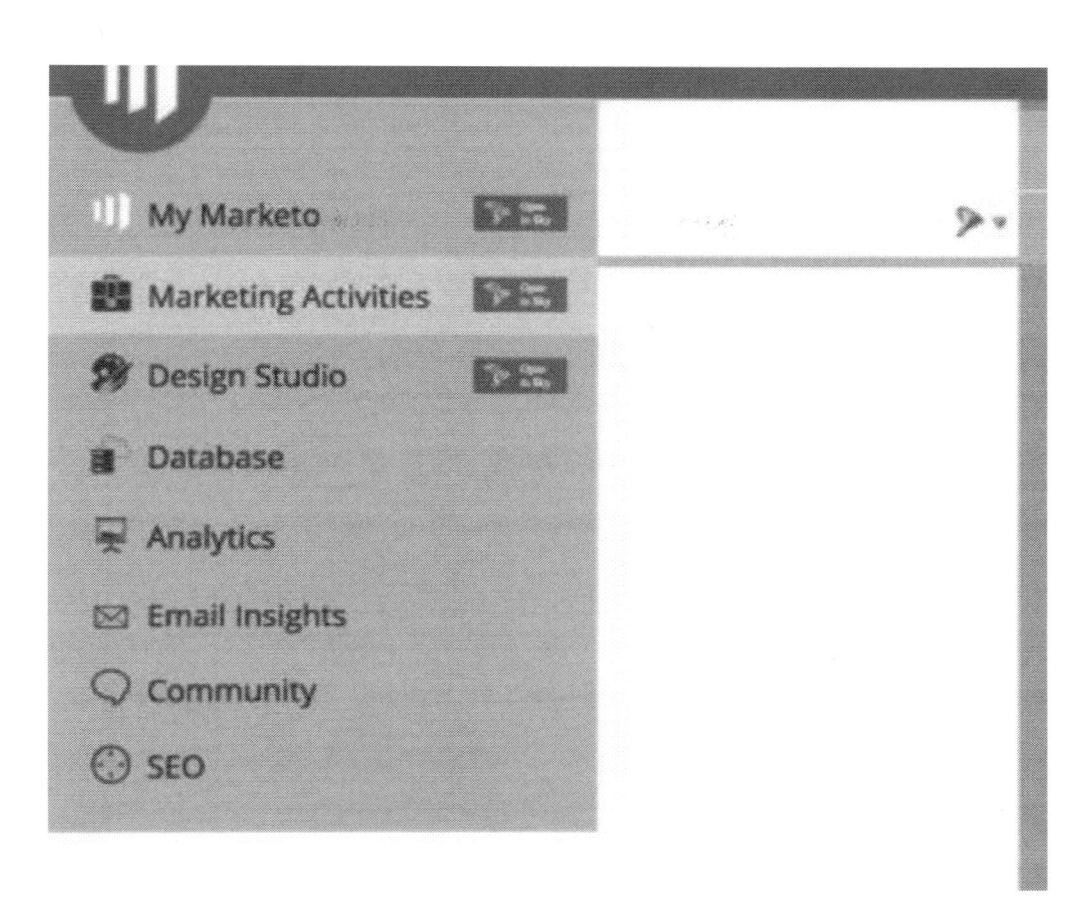

It's recommended you start off with the following structure, or something along the same lines for your organization's needs specifically:

Active Marketing Activities (Parent Folder)

- Emails – (Sub-folders)

- Newsletters

- Nurture Programs

- Ads/PPC

- Web Content

- Web Forms
- List Imports
- Events
    - Live Events / Roadshows
    - Tradeshows
    - Webinars

Operational Programs (Parent Folder)

- Data Management (Sub-folders)
- Scoring
- Subscription center
- **_Archive Folder (Parent Folder)**

```
▼ 📁 Marketing Activities
  ▼ 📁 Active Marketing Programs
      📁 Emails
    ▼ 📁 Events
        📁 Live Events / Roadshows
        📁 Trade Shows
        📁 Webinars
      📁 List Imports
      📁 Newsletters
      📁 Nurture
      📁 Web Content
      📁 Web Forms
  ▶ 📁 Marketo Program Templates
  ▶ 📁 Operational
  ▶ 📁 Sales Insight
      📁 Z Archive
```

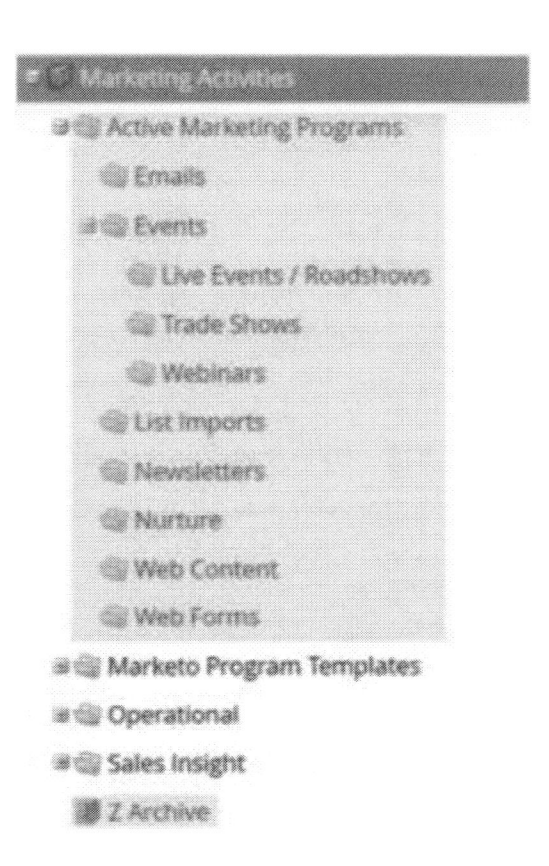

Active Marketing Activities

It's important to consider our current and most active marketing programs from the top. Create a parent folder that has a broad, easy-to-understand name which indicates what is within. Once it expands, name each subfolder by the channel your marketing programs belong to. I've listed some examples above that you can use as a starting point. Your marketing programs and everything associated will live in their respective folders. Notice how the events folder has subfolders for different types of events. These should help you in thinking about how you can create other subfolders for where they would be helpful. You may be buying ads from Google, Facebook, or LinkedIn. It would be helpful to structure your PPC programs as such. The key here is to use good judgment while keeping in mind creating an easy-to-navigate experience for any new admins in the future.

Operational Folder

Your operational folder should have everything "non-marketing" related within it. This includes your data management programs, person source tracking, scoring, data normalization campaigns, subscription center, and everything that's needed to ensure things are running smoothly in the background. We will talk about operational programs in the next chapter in more detail.

Archive Folder

Lastly, it's vital to have an archived folder. In fact, I will re-emphasize it in each section to drive the point home! The earlier you get into the habit of archiving old programs, unused campaigns, assets, and test data, etc., the cleaner your instance will be and the better experience you and your team will have! I've come across many users who delete assets that were no longer in use. That proved to be a problem for lots of marketing teams who then expected to run a quick email-performance report and realized one of their newsletters, or a quarter's worth of newsletters were deleted. Yikes! To prevent that from happening, archiving your folders will allow you to essentially hide them from view and still be able to report on them! A quick tip with all archive folders is to add an underscore or a lower-case letter "z" in front of the name. Since everything is sorted alphanumerically in the Marketo-tree (toward the left of the Marketo screen), adding either of these characters to the front of the name will push that folder down, out of view and out of mind. This goes for any folder or program you'd like to push toward the lower parts of the screen to make room for what's more important.

The next major benefit of cleaning up as you go, aside from not having to delete anything to keep your reporting intact, is the ability to find the most relevant assets required. What archiving will do is it will "hide" folders, programs, campaigns, and assets from your daily view. It will also prevent them from appearing in any picklists. For example, when you build a smart campaign and need to use the email flow step, imagine having to sift through hundreds of emails. Even if you start typing to search for exact ones, there could be others that could distract you that appear. By archiving unused & old folders with program & assets, you're able to accelerate the time it takes you and your team to find what's truly important at that time. Below is a screenshot of an archive folder, toward the bottom, that should be used in all sections where applicable:

- CO-Active Marketing Programs
- CO-Communities Website
- CO-Emails
- CO-Nurture
- CO-Program Samples
- CO-Newsletters
- CO-Events
- CO-Web Forms
- CO-Web Content
- CO-Z-Learning
- CO-ZZ-Archive

Design Studio

Next, we'll jump into the design studio. This is where all of your global assets will live. It's important to create folders for each category of assets, landing pages, emails, forms, snippets, and files & images.

For each of the assets, emphasize the difference between global assets vs. local assets that will be located in the marketing activities section. **Global assets will be reusable amongst other programs and campaigns while local assets are those tied to one particular marketing program**. An example of a global form could be your website's contact-us form. Sure, it's used on your website, but you can leverage the same form on other individual landing pages when directing someone to fill out a similar form. This helps save tons of time by not having to create forms from scratch.

The foldering structure that's recommended for the Design Studio should look something similar to the following:

- **Landing Pages**
  - Global Landing Pages
  - Templates (MKTO-seeded folder)
  - _Archive
- **Emails**
  - Global Emails
  - Templates (MKTO-seeded folder)
  - _Archive
- **Forms**
  - Global Forms
  - _Archive

- **Snippets**
  - _Archive
- **Files & Images**
  - Logos
  - Banners
  - PDFs
  - _Archive

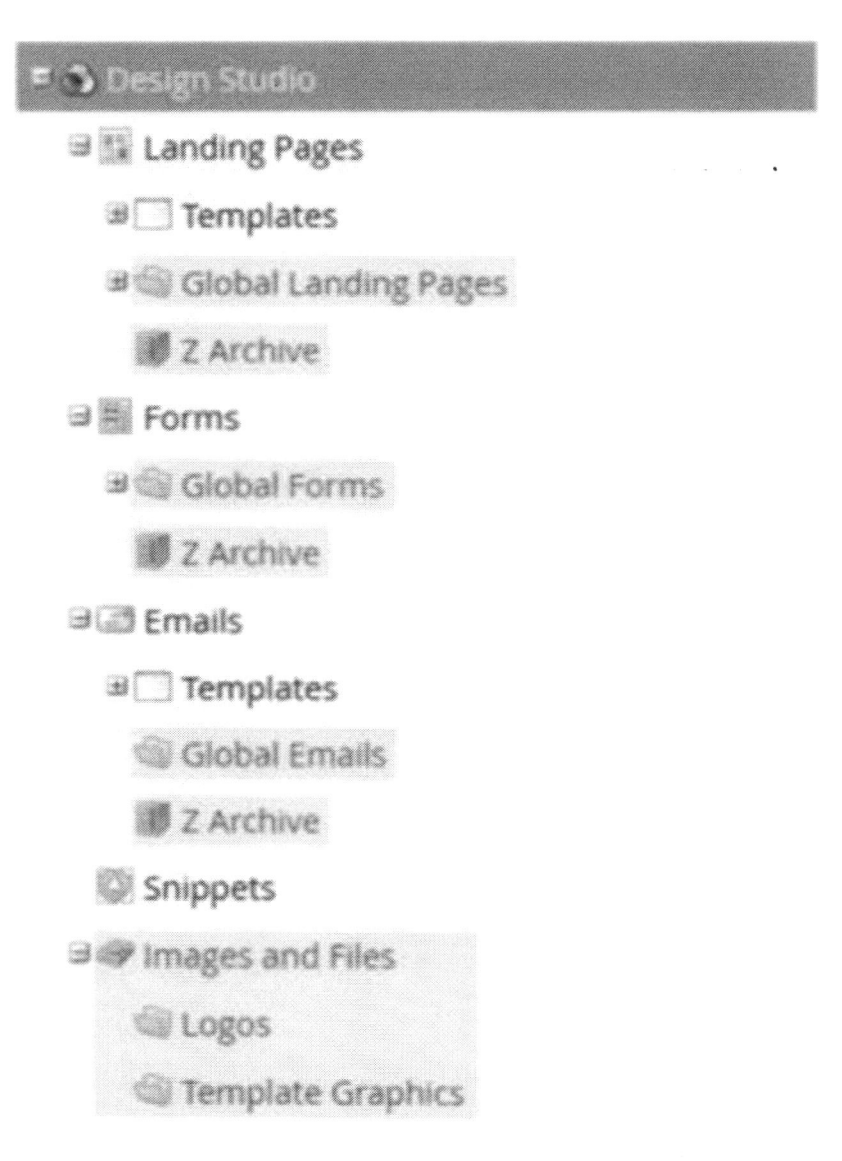

```
⊟ 🌐 Design Studio
    ⊟ 🗔 Landing Pages
        ⊞ ☐ Templates
        ⊞ 📁 Global Landing Pages
            📦 Z Archive
    ⊟ 🗔 Forms
        ⊞ 📁 Global Forms
            📦 Z Archive
    ⊟ 📁 Emails
        ⊞ ☐ Templates
            📁 Global Emails
            📦 Z Archive
        🌐 Snippets
    ⊟ 📁 Images and Files
        📁 Logos
        📁 Template Graphics
```

Of course, you can add other subfolders that make sense for your organization. Just keep in mind the concept of global assets when creating these and that the same asset could be used in multiple places. So, if you want to separate your assets by types of channels they'll be used for, that may help everyone who may be looking to find a specific asset for an upcoming webinar, as an example.

Creating an archive folder in the Design studio is no different! There will be dozens, if not hundreds of assets that you will accumulate over time. Most you'll probably need once or twice, which makes archiving even more critical. I see this way too much with many organizations where 500 landing pages, 400 emails, 150 forms, etc., litter their design studio causing unpleasant experiences for any marketing-ops person who just needs to build a required program as soon as possible.

Database

The next section we'll discuss is the database where all of your leads & contacts reside! Marketo does a great job offering some system smart-lists here to get you thinking about how to segment your audiences. These reside in a pre-seeded folder simply titled "System Smart-lists".

There are three main folders in this section as well. One of them is "Segmentations," which we'll leave for a later chapter when we discuss dynamic content. The other two are "Group Smart Lists" and "Group Lists." I'm not going to get into the specifics of each but basically smart-lists are dynamic lists that allow you to filter your database using various sets of filtering options such as simple fields (i.e., country field, email domain, etc.) or activity fields (i.e., Clicked Link in Email, Visited Webpage, etc.). Group Lists are simply buckets of leads/contacts that don't have any filtering associated with them. You can simply upload a list of people and they'll be included in their own list henceforth.

For foldering and naming best-practices in the database I recommend the below structure to get started with. Of course, and as mentioned earlier, the following are simple examples and should be expanded on when thinking about your own organization.

- **My Smart lists (Parent Folder)**

- Exclusion Lists
  - Competitors
  - Employees
  - Partners
- Operational
  - Marketable Persons
- _Archive
- **My Lists (Parent Folder)**
- Internal
- _Archive

- Lead Database
  - System Smart Lists
  - My Smart Lists
    - Exclusion Lists
    - Operational Lists
    - Z Archive
  - My Lists
    - Internal Lists
    - Z Archive
  - Segmentations

For the **My Smart Lists**, it's recommended that you start off with some exclusion lists. The can include competitors, your internal employees, and even 3rd party partners, vendors, etc., should be considered. I don't want to go off track too far, but I'd like to pause here to discuss two recommended smart-lists that I've seen be invaluable to many organizations.

(1) The **Competitors Smart-List** will be needed in the next chapter to black-list any companies that you'll consider a competitor who enters Marketo. There are two filters that should be used here to create this list:

- **Email Address** – Should have a "contains" operator and consider organizations who may have different email domains from their company names (i.e. Kaiser Permanente vs. kp.org).

- **Company name** – Should also have a "contains" operator to capture any variations of how competitor names are added to that specific field.

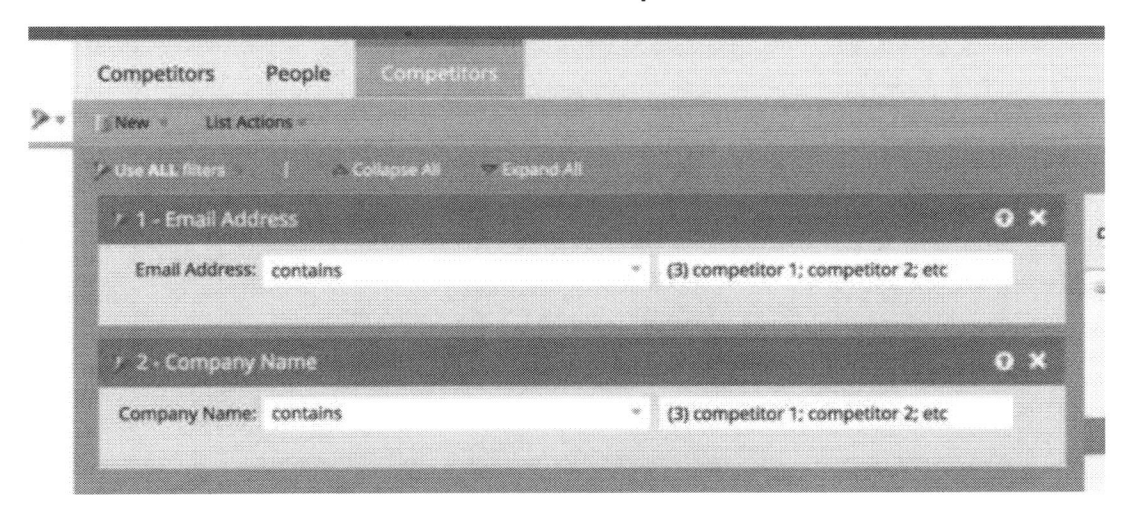

(2) The **Marketable Persons Smart-List** is vital for email programs. It's used as a suppression list within a smart

campaign to prevent people who aren't marketable to enter any flow steps. I'll provide an example of the filters that should be used to create this, and more context as to why it's a best practice to leverage this in your email programs/campaigns.

- In this smart list, include the following filter logic:
  - **Unsubscribed** = False
  - **Marketing Suspended** = False
  - **Blacklisted** = False
  - **Email Invalid** = False
  - **Email Address** – contains = @ and a period (.)

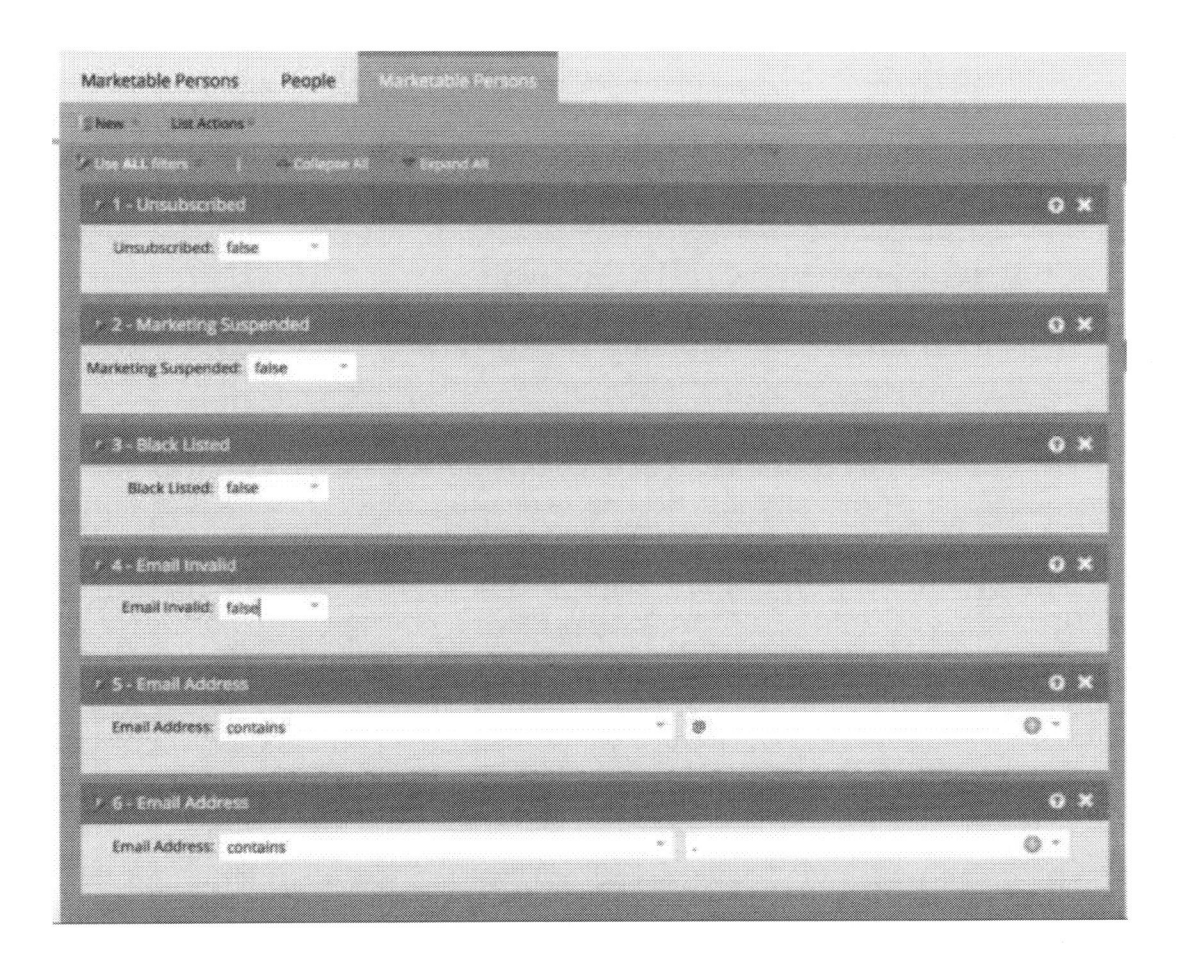

The answer to "why" this is important when it comes to email campaigns is simple! Marketo does a phenomenal job by preventing emails being sent to anyone that either has one of the above fields set to True or if their email is not a valid email to send to. But, where this starts to break down is when you have a program, or even a single smart-campaign that has an email flow step in it, **followed by other custom flow steps** such as "Change Data Value", "Add to list", "Sync to SFDC campaign", etc., Let's assume that the "Marketable Persons" smart-list is not used in the campaign's logic. If people who have, for example, unsubscribed = True, qualify for the campaign they will proceed into the flow step and YES, they will skip the email flow-step since they are unsubscribed. But they will then proceed to any other flow-steps you've added where they will have an unnecessary data-value-change to a field(s), be added to the wrong list, and will sync to your SFDC campaigns which will all have a potential impact on your reporting metrics and possibly poorer data hygiene.

The **Archive Folder** in the smart-list portion of the database is different from the other areas in Marketo. Smart-lists, in and of themselves, are always turned on and constantly listening for people that enter Marketo who match the criteria of the filters used inside of them, even if it just listened and queried the database for the same information a few seconds ago. We'll discuss this in the next chapter when exploring segmentations and dynamic content, but to sum it up, having hundreds of smart-lists querying the system on top of all the other programs and campaigns you may have running can be a drain on Marketo. Archiving won't help here because even if you archive, the constant querying will continue! You'll need to either remove the filters to make the smart list blank or delete it. Be careful of the latter option in the event that smart-list is being used in other campaigns or programs. The only aspect of archiving smart lists that's helpful is that they will be removed from any picklists. So, if you feel like some thoroughly built robust smart-lists aren't worth tossing just yet, archiving them for future use can be life-saving.

For the **Group lists**, it's recommended to create subfolders based on what these "buckets" of people are used for. In most cases, these are uploaded lists for internal use. Creating an archiving folder for this asset is helpful because this is one asset-type that's **least often** re-used, and more importantly least often deleted. This can add tons of clutter to your instance really quick and the best-practice for cleaning up static-lists is cleaning up as you go.

Analytics

In Marketo's Analytics section, there are two seeded folders, "My Reports" which when saving a report is only visible to the creator. And, "Group Reports" which are visible to everyone who has access to this section of Marketo. A helpful way to think about foldering here is by breaking them down based on what's being reported. For example:

- **Group Reports** – (Parent Folder)
  - Web Activity
  - By Person Source
  - Program Performance
  - Email Performance

There are other types of reports that are available in this section, but by creating subfolders for each, it's easy for anyone who logs in to find the reports they need quickly.

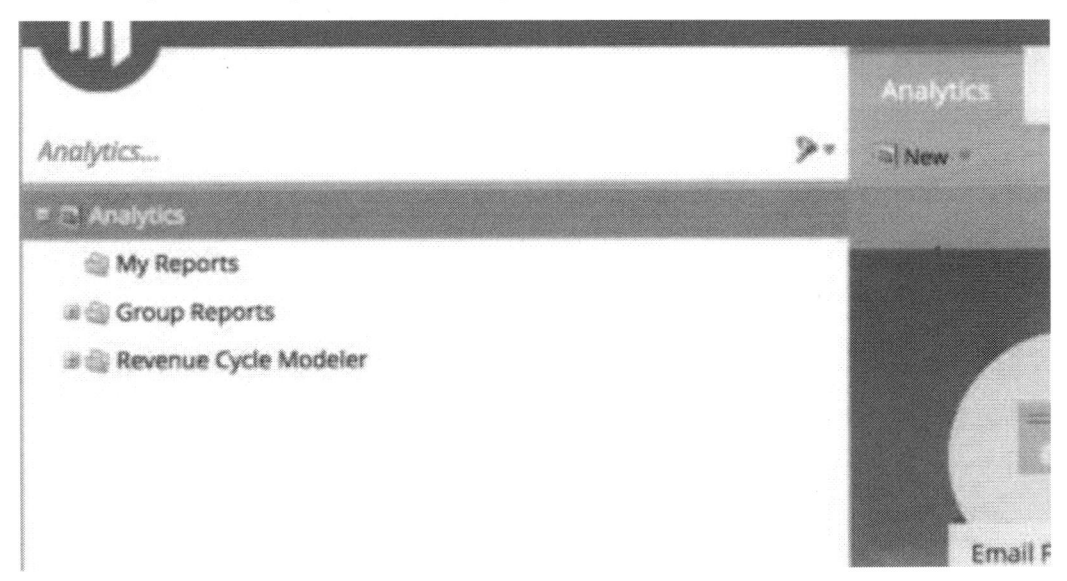

Now that we've talked about a good foldering strategy, it's time to focus on naming conventions.

Program Naming Convention

The main reason you'll want to standardize a naming convention for your programs is for reporting. Marketo is a great tool, but its Program Performance report has a few nuances that can prove to be frustrating later on if a naming convention is not followed. Below is a screenshot of a program performance report of what we are hoping to avoid:

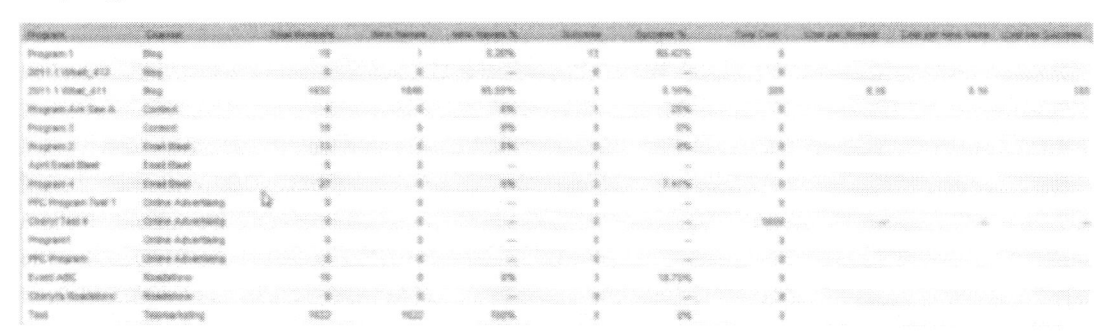

If no strategic format is followed in your program names, you'll have a mixed list of jumbled programs that would frustrate even the most patient of marketers who just need to get a report out the door. The problem with Marketo's program performance report is the lack of ability to filter by program **name**, which makes things a bit tough. Imagine you have 100+ programs, and no way to filter your report based on, for example, only webinar programs that

were on the east coast in 2018? Instead, you have to cherry-pick them in a sea of other program names. What we want is something that looks like the below:

You'll notice that when looking at the above report, a recommended best-practice program naming convention follows the format:

[Abbreviation of Program Type] [YYYY]-[MM]-[Optional DD] [Brief Description]

Example – WBN-2016-11-16-Weekly Webinar

This way, when your programs appear in the program performance report, they will all alphanumerically sort (as mentioned earlier). You're using the alphanumeric sorting to your advantage along with creating a standardized format for your organization to follow, making your programs really easy to find! The key things to keep in mind when thinking about a program naming convention are the following:

(1) Make them short, but as long as necessary. A benefit with starting with the channel acronym is that when searching for programs in pick lists, you only need to type in "WBN" to narrow your search down to one particular channel of programs, in this case, webinars.

(2) If you create long program names, keep in mind the pitfalls & drawbacks include slowing down your day-to-day operations. Marketo will display the program in your picklists with three little dots (…) toward the right of each program name in the drop-down, requiring you to click the corner of the picklist and drag it out to see the full name (to ensure you're referencing the correct program). Imagine doing this 20-times a day, day after day (needing to drag the right corner each and every time you're creating a campaign). Trust me when I say this saves you time!

(3) Do not add periods into your program name. The reason is that Marketo will display your assets when you are searching for them in picklists by program-name first followed by a period, and then the asset name (see below example). if you

have multiple periods in your program name it will cause confusion amongst your team as people will wonder where is the asset name start? Where does the program name end? To avoid this, avoid using periods in the program name!

Example: WBN-2016-11-16-Weekly Webinar.**Invitation**

(4) Add any additional customizations for your own organization. Be creative but use good judgment as to what makes sense for your company's business. One good way to think about how to customize the best-practice program naming convention is by using Geo-location, product lines, business units, etc., in front of the name. Below is an example of how you can customize your programs for your organization specifically using geo-location:

Example: **EMEA**-WBN-2016-11-16-Weekly Webinar

Customizing the naming convention to include different global regions will allow you to report on your programs by which marketing teams in APAC, EMEA, etc., are running them.

Below I've put together a quick cheat-sheet for consideration

[Abbreviation of Program Type] [YYYY]-[MM]-[Optional DD] [Brief Description]

- CS - Content Syndication
- EB - Email Blast
- ES - Email Send
- ENG - Engagement Program
- LE - Live Event
- LI - List Import
- NL - Newsletter
- OA - Online Advertising
- PPC - Pay Per Click
- TS - Tradeshow
- WBN - Webinar
- WC - Website Content

Smart-Campaign Naming Convention

Smart campaigns are instrumental in Marketo. They are what make your marketing programs work the way you desire and are one of the most critical automation tools in the platform. What's even more important is the ability to troubleshoot them when something's not working the way you expected. Or even worse, you just joined a new team or inherited a new Marketo instance and an old legacy campaign that's been running into an issue. If you're lucky job that day is to troubleshoot it and if your predecessor didn't have a good naming convention, it'll make it tough to pinpoint what campaign is causing what.

The naming convention recommended for smart campaigns will help alleviate this issue, along with accelerating your pick-list values and scaling your programs into templates that can be easily cloned.

Start by using the following format:

"Numerical Digit – Brief Description"

Or

"01-Send Invitations"

Using a numerical digit at the front of your campaign name will allow Marketo's alphanumerical sorting to structure your programs campaigns in a way that tells a story. Take the below webinar and nurture program examples:

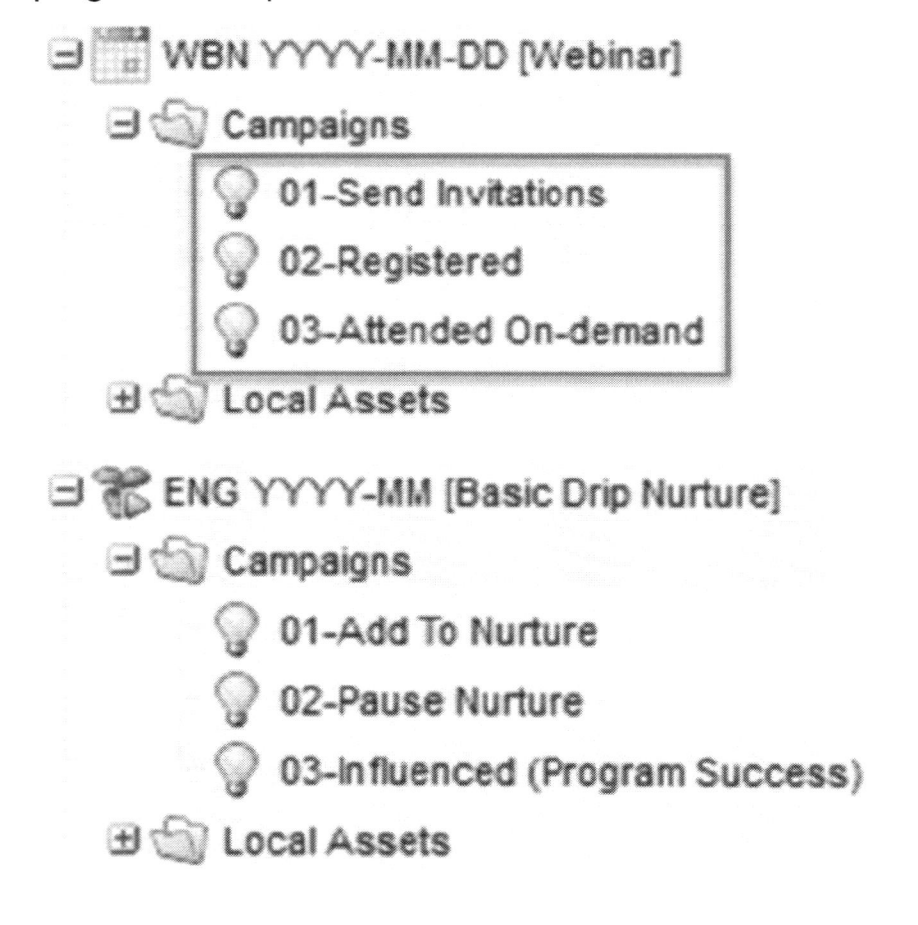

- WBN YYYY-MM-DD [Webinar]
    - Campaigns
        - 01-Send Invitations
        - 02-Registered
        - 03-Attended On-demand
    - Local Assets
- ENG YYYY-MM [Basic Drip Nurture]
    - Campaigns
        - 01-Add To Nurture
        - 02-Pause Nurture
        - 03-Influenced (Program Success)
    - Local Assets

You can see that the first campaign that's set to run is the invitation to the webinar. The 2nd is the campaign that processes

registrations, and lastly, the 3rd campaign will stamp a record as a "success", or having a prospect reach the goal of that marketing program, if the invitee(s) attended.

The benefits of structuring your smart campaigns using the above format are that anyone who opens a campaigns folder can easily understand the sequence of events that will occur. It's easier to pinpoint the correct source of an issue that may arise in one of the campaigns, for example, if the confirmation email needs to be replaced or an additional step needs to be added/removed. As your team grows, it'll be even more crucial to provide new members an easy way to navigate through the programs you've created, not to mention your managers and leadership team.

The next items to keep in mind is ensuring your description is relatively short, if possible. This will speed up the time it takes to find the correct campaign in pick lists when building campaigns. We mentioned this briefly earlier, but it helps to emphasize that in all Marketo asset naming.

Lastly, keep your smart campaign names neutral! This means, do not give specific detailed names but rather create them for the purpose of cloning the program in the future. For example, take the below webinar program again:

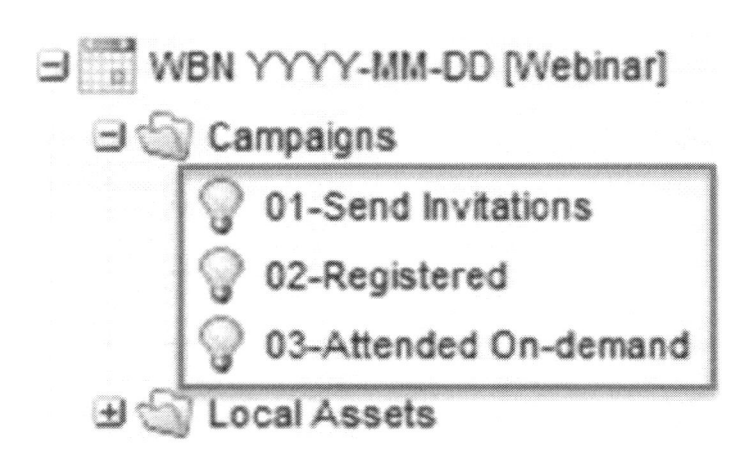

```
□ 🗓 WBN YYYY-MM-DD [Webinar]
   □ 📁 Campaigns
       💡 01-Send Invitations
       💡 02-Registered
       💡 03-Attended On-demand
   ⊞ 📁 Local Assets
```

By keeping the campaign name descriptions as Send Invitation, Registered, & Attended, you'll be able to clone the same program and save time by not renaming the campaign names again. Let's face it, a webinar program's structure is not going to change too often. You'll always send out an invite, maybe now include reminders, and will always process registrations. By keeping the names neutral, you'll be able to clone and get another program running more quickly without having to go back and make additional edits to the initial campaign names!

Lastly, do not include periods in your smart campaign names for the same reasons as mentioned earlier. And, do not repeat the program name in the campaign name. This is where marketing-ops teams create lots of confusion by trying to tie a campaign name to a specific program. But again, keep in mind that your pick-lists will display campaigns that you search for using the format **"program name.campaign name"**, so it will be confusing to see duplicate programs names, not to mention long detailed names.

Asset Naming Convention

When we referring to Marketo assets and program assets, we're referring to the different emails, templates, landing pages, forms, images and files associated with your Marketo programs. The purpose of having a strategic naming convention for assets is to locate them quickly when referencing them in filters, triggers, other programs, and pretty much anywhere in Marketo.

You can see there are names that may have periods or numbers, some are upper case and others are lower case and it's really difficult to quickly pinpoint which is the correct asset that you need! The above screenshot is something we are hoping to stay away from. The recommended naming convention for all assets is the following format:

"**ASSET TYPE**-Short Description"

EMAIL-invitation (for email assets)
LP-registration (for landing pages)
FORM-registration (for forms)
SLIST-attended (for smart lists)

The above examples help with two main benefits. First, your ability to quickly group all relevant assets next to each other when they're in a folder. This is immensely helpful when building out large programs that have lots of emails, landing pages, etc. What we don't want for ourselves is to open a folder and see random names next to each asset icon and hope we can make heads or tails as to what asset is which. By following the above naming convention, you should be able to build large programs and Marketo's alphanumeric sorting will help with organizing your assets, so they're easily found. Below is an example of a Live Event program that consists of several different assets:

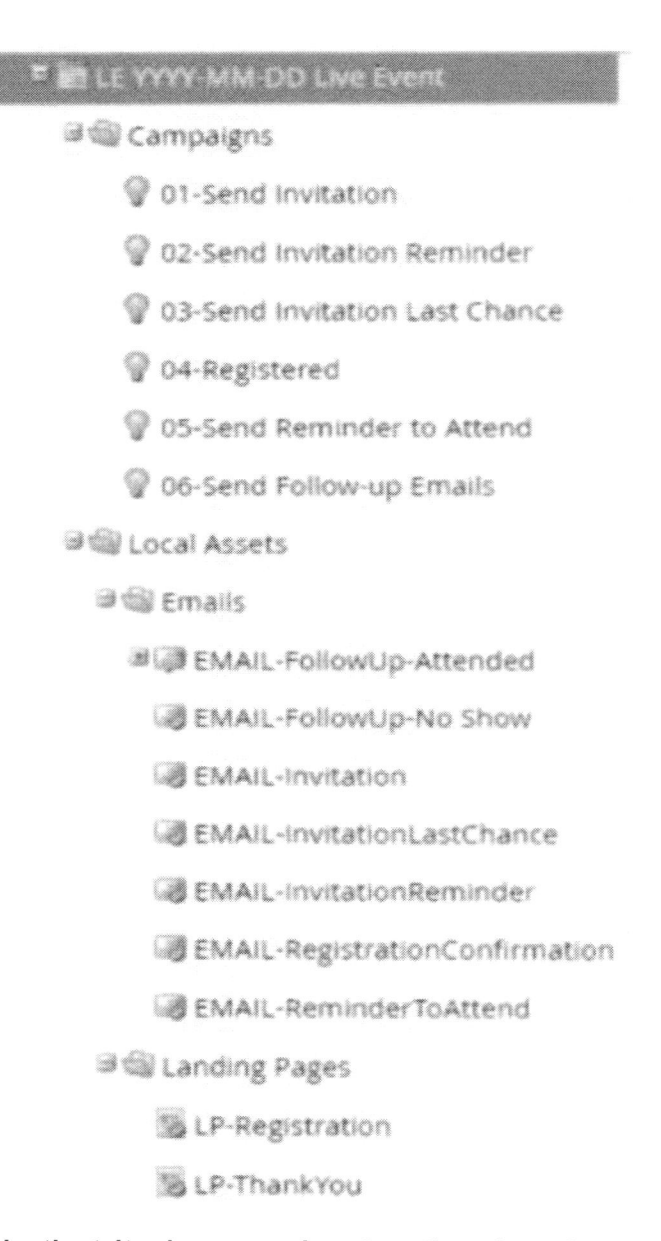

```
▼ 📅 LE YYYY-MM-DD Live Event
    ▣ 📁 Campaigns
        💡 01-Send Invitation
        💡 02-Send Invitation Reminder
        💡 03-Send Invitation Last Chance
        💡 04-Registered
        💡 05-Send Reminder to Attend
        💡 06-Send Follow-up Emails
    ▣ 📁 Local Assets
        ▣ 📁 Emails
            📧 EMAIL-FollowUp-Attended
            📧 EMAIL-FollowUp-No Show
            📧 EMAIL-Invitation
            📧 EMAIL-InvitationLastChance
            📧 EMAIL-InvitationReminder
            📧 EMAIL-RegistrationConfirmation
            📧 EMAIL-ReminderToAttend
        ▣ 📁 Landing Pages
            📄 LP-Registration
            📄 LP-ThankYou
```

The 2nd benefit is that it also accelerates the time it takes to comb through pick-lists to find the actual asset you're looking for. For instance, let's say we're building out a campaign and need to reference a **landing page** that was built for an event. That asset's name is given a generic "Registration" title, to keep things neutral (again for cloning purposes). If I type the name of the landing page into a filter or trigger, I may also see **forms or other assets** with the word "registration" in the title from other marketing programs. By adding the asset type in capital letters at the front of the asset name, I can quickly pinpoint the correct asset-type so that I can get on with my day to more important things.

In conclusion and a key takeaway from this chapter is that those Marketo customers who implement a strategic naming convention are those that create a pleasant experience for themselves from the get-go! Those who don't will find it to be a cluttered pain-in-the-you-know-where to use. Start off with the right foot forward, OR start looking at the instance you currently own and consider the benefits of incorporating the naming conventions discussed in this chapter. Your team will appreciate, and your boss will love the initiative!

Chapter 2 - Operational Programs & Data Management

Now that we understand how to think about naming folders and programs, the next vital component of any implementation is operational programs! For those who don't know what these are or haven't quite heard the term, operational programs are any non-marketing programs that are running in the background, normalizing field values, scoring leads, and even checking if emails are bouncing and ensuring that your email domain's reputation isn't negatively affected. There are several others that can be created, and we'll discuss some of them in this chapter.

- **Operational Folder**

As you've probably gathered by now, it's important to keep your Marketo instance consistent and organized. For this reason, you'll want to ensure that there is a separate folder dedicated to all things operational. This should be a parent folder, and all subsequent operational programs should reside in subfolders for easy navigation. Below, we'll start off with the common must-have operational programs that majority of all Marketo teams consider and employ.

- Creating a **Person Source** strategy

The first step to creating this type of program will be creating a person source *strategy*. Typically, most marketing teams want to know which channels are acquiring, or sourcing, their leads the best, as well as the worst. This is where two fields in Marketo come in handy.

Through the initial provisioning of your Marketo instance, there is a Marketo field created called "**Acquisition Program**". Keep in mind that this field gets stamped automatically in *most cases*, such as when a new lead enters into Marketo through an asset associated with a Marketo program. You should also have the field "**Source**", which should be mapped to your CRM's lead source field. If you don't already, consider creating one or leveraging the one Marketo offers out of the box. Ensure that your organization's correct fields are used when proceeding with the below best practice configuration.

(1) First, create a parent folder titled "Operational Programs". Then, right-click on the folder and create a subfolder called "Person Source". Then, right click on the subfolder and select "Create Program". You'll want to create a new *default* program titled "Person Source" and tie it to the "Operational" channel as shown below:

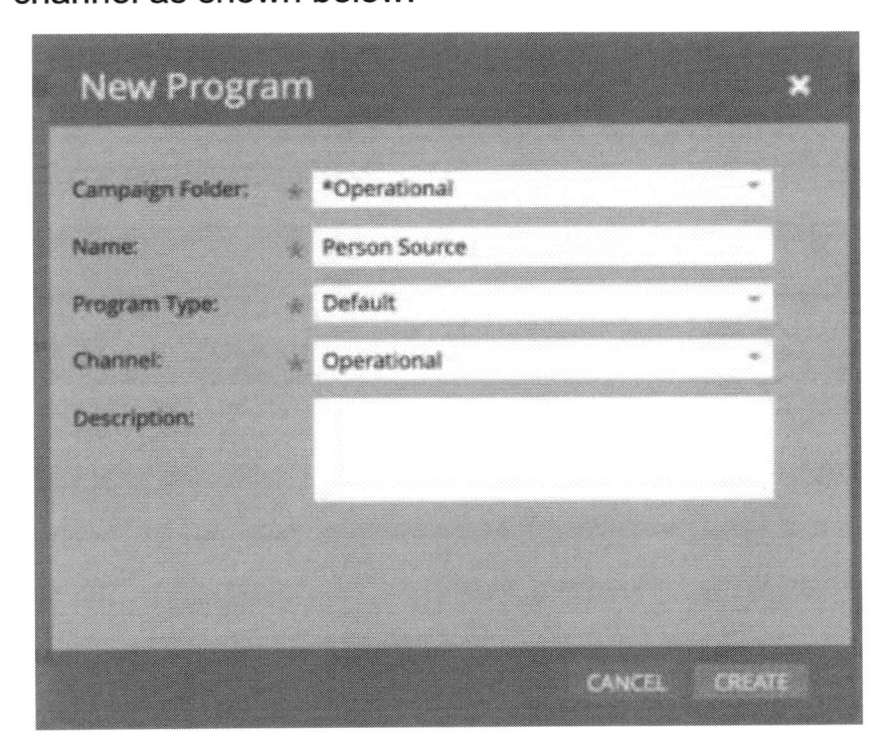

Campaign Folder:	*Operational
Name:	Person Source
Program Type:	Default
Channel:	Operational
Description:	

(2) Under the program, create a subfolder called "campaigns". Then, create your first campaign that will stamp the aforementioned source field(s). Below is an example of how the smart-list and flow tab should be set up for a ***very simple*** configuration that depends on webinar-sourced-leads to come from the registration form:

Name: Source by Webinar

Smart List Tab Criteria

(1) Trigger = person is created (& constraint is "Form Name contains "WBN") + (another constraint for Person Source **is empty**)

(2) Filter = Unsubscribe = False

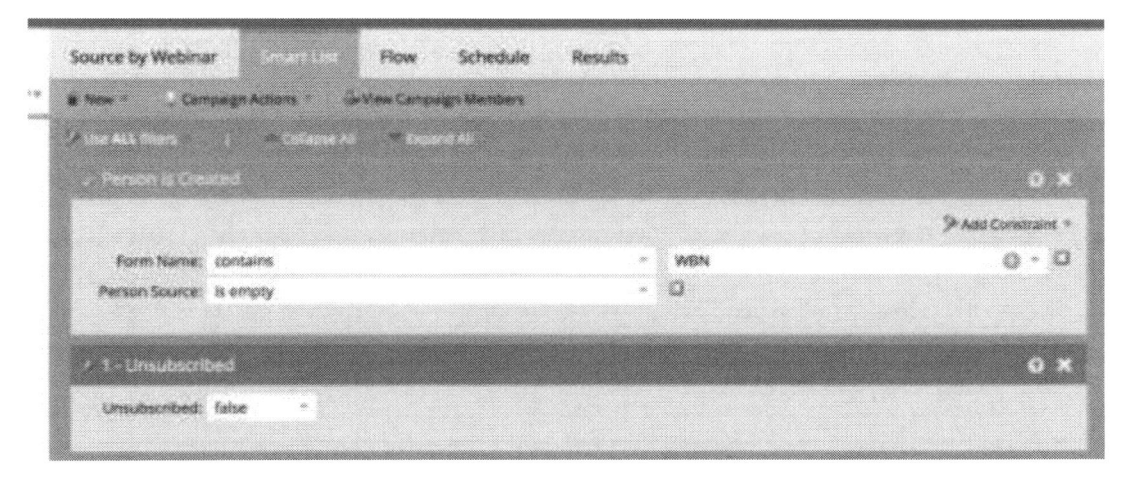

Flow Tab Criteria:

(1) Change Data Value - (Attribute is "Person Source" and new value = "Webinar")

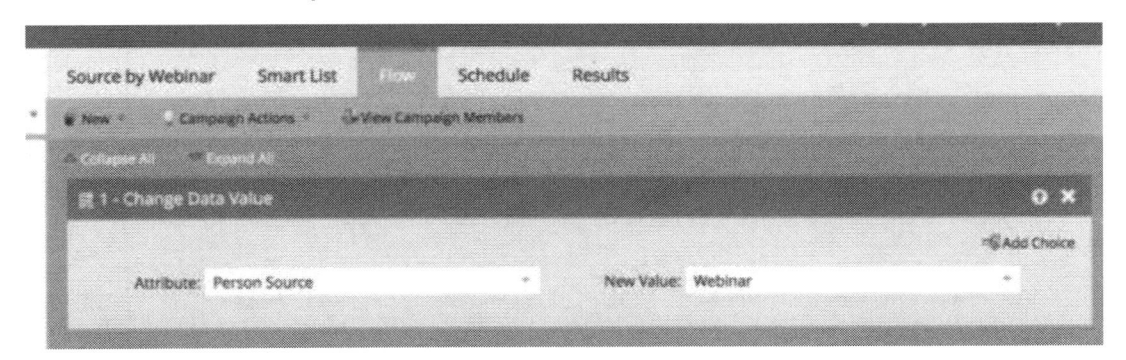

Then once the above campaign has been set up, **clone the campaign for as many channels that you will be creating marketing programs** for that can acquire net-new leads. For example, thinking about lead acquisition programs such as events, gated content, and pretty much any that have a form related to them, you'll want to create a **separate campaign** for each. Simply swap out the smart list criteria so that instead of "WBN" in the example used above, you're using the abbreviation suggested in the first chapter for the other channels you will be marketing through. For example, LE (live event), TS (trade show), WC (web-content) etc.,

Using these operational campaigns to stamp source fields is invaluable in deciphering which channels are acquiring leads the best quarter after quarter. You can create a report to determine which channel brings in the most, and the least, net-new records. In addition to the person source fields, you also have Marketo's "**acquisition program**" field which will allow you to report on the best of both worlds.

What do I mean by "best of both worlds" exactly? Using the "**source**" field that your organization uses in these campaigns, you will be able to report on which channels acquire leads. With the "**acquisition program**" field, you're able to drill down to determine which programs *within each channel* have the most lead acquisition. This will help you determine what's working, and what's not for all channels.

Now that we have the purpose of why creating a lead strategy is important, along with the campaign structure in place, let's discuss two best practices that will take your strategy even further!

First, it's critical that if this hasn't been done yet, you navigate to your admin section within your instance and **block** the person source field from getting overwritten. To accomplish this, navigate to Admin > Field Management. Then, search for the source field in the right search area and when found click on "Field Actions" in the top left corner, as shown below, and select "Block Field Updates":

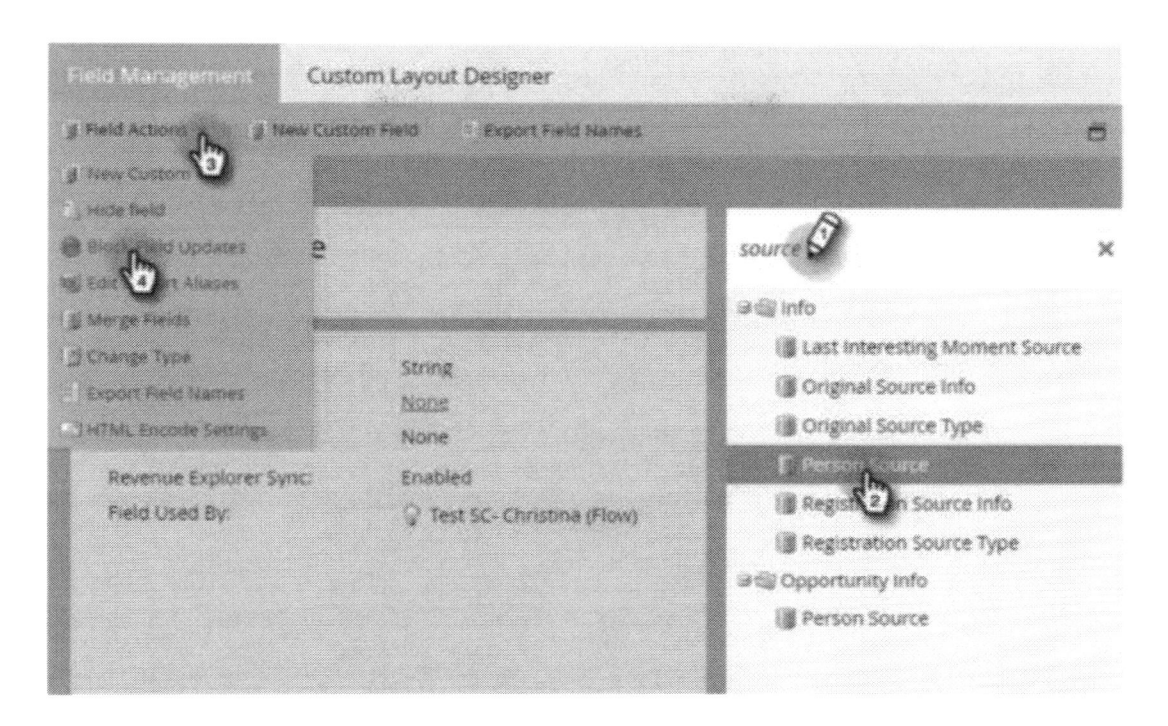

Ensure that this is blocked from all of the appropriate options. This will prevent the same field from updating if the same lead/person fills out another form after already getting acquired into Marketo.

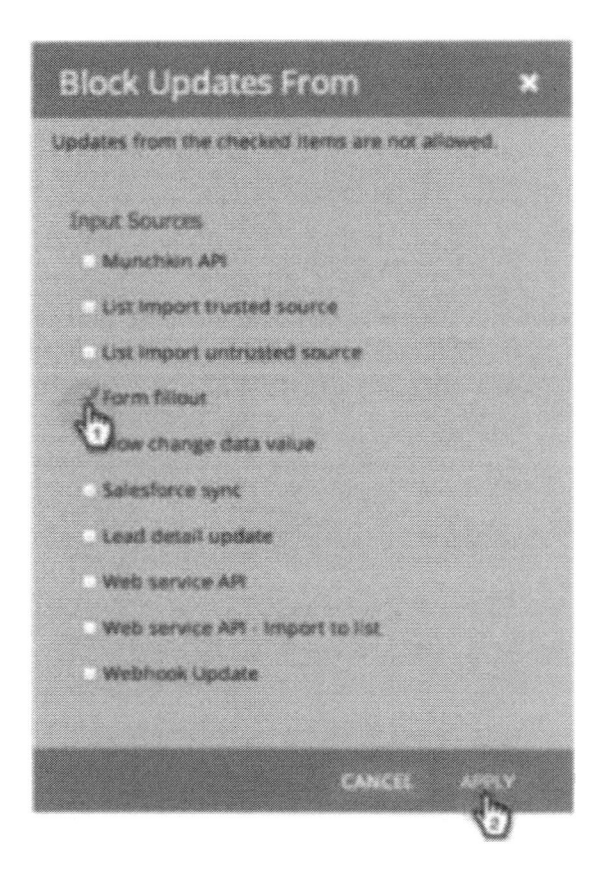

Another best-practice you'll want to consider is creating another separate custom field for "**Most Recent Source**". This field should be blocked from being overwritten and its purpose is to track the same leads **last-touch**. You may already be guessing, but this second field will **not** need to be blocked from getting overwritten as it will continuously overwrite itself based on the last program a lead engages with.

What will occur is every time a lead interacts with any program, a campaign in that program will have a data-value-change flow step that will update this field. It's critical that if it's decided to use this type of field, that you think of a strategic way to stamp this field in a scalable way.

I recommend two methods. The first is through any program-template where you have a flow step created to stamp this field. That way, when you clone the program template to reuse again, you don't have to worry about forgetting to add this change-data-value flow-step when building new programs. The second way is to create a hidden field on your forms that will auto-stamp the "most recent source field" upon submission. It's worth noting that this method should supplement the first as it allows you to operationally use forms to capture "most recent source" but other campaigns should still capture important milestones not related to forms, such as event attendance, email success reached etc. Using forms' hidden fields to solely capture "most recent source" creates room for human error if, and when, someone forgets to add it to a new form.

- Data Normalization Campaigns -

The next program is meant to keep your data hygiene squeaky clean. I'll use two examples to illustrate how this can be created for any "dirty" hygiene fields you may have in your CRM. For example, let's use the State and Country fields.

There could be dozens, if not more, ways that someone could enter the word "USA". Sure, it's best practice to standardize the options people can select in a form using a pick list. But what about your CRM users. Are you confident in your sales users entering a standard abbreviation of "USA"? I don't think so, at least not the majority of them. Same goes for US states. Think of how many variations you may have seen the word California?

The problem that arise when having multiple values in such fields can lead to skewed reporting, incorrect lead scoring, and faulty smart campaigns that depend on these fields. Imagine trying to run a report for your executive team on how many net-new people came from your US territory? If you don't think or guess **ALL** the different variations states in your territory are entered into CRM, you risk providing a skewed report. Think about your demographic lead scoring that you may have currently, or will be building soon, which will discuss in a later chapter. There's more risk in possibly missing leads that ought to have been scored because they were not included in your territory due to a simple spelling error, such as U.SA vs. USA. I recommend every organization go through the short exercise of thinking of 3 or 4 "dirty" hygiene fields they know are present in their CRM, and create the below campaigns for them:

Smart List Tab Criteria

(1) Filter- Country (Field) "contains" = us, U.s.a, USA, United state, US of A, etc., (either think of all the different variations or create a quick report in CRM to find most commonly used values and paste them into the filter shown in the screenshot below)

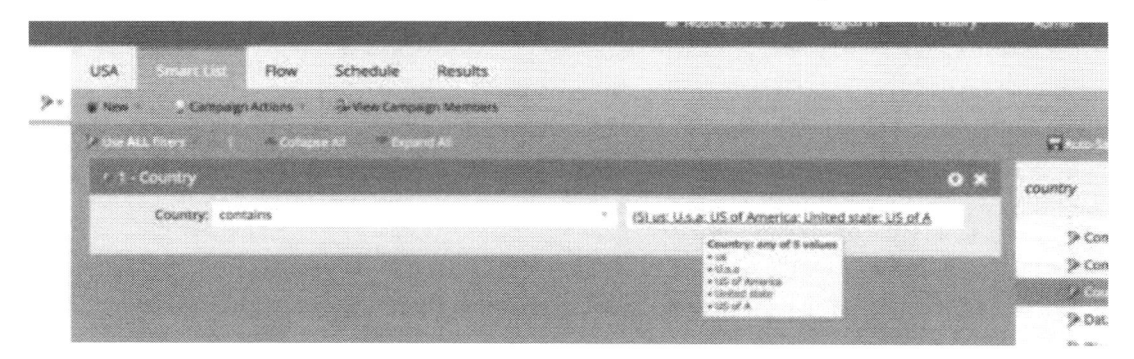

Flow Tab Criteria:

(1) Change Data Value (Flow Step) of "Country" field = USA

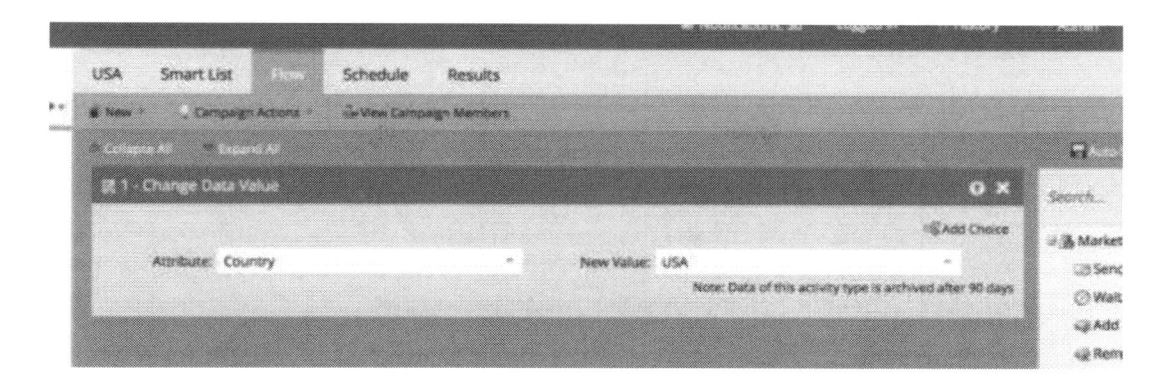

Schedule Tab Criteria:

Set this as a recurring batch campaign by selecting "**Schedule Recurrence**" to run nightly at 2am (or any late hour), preventing any interference with more important marketing campaigns scheduled to run during the day.

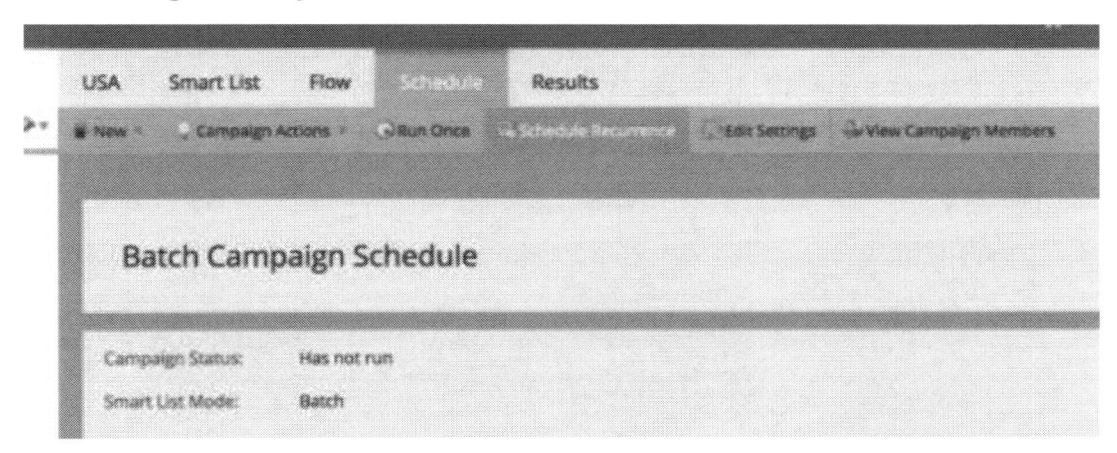

The same concept applies to the state field, department, industry, title, etc., Imagine how many different variations you have seen of "CEO" or something similar. By standardizing a select few fields that need some cleanup, you're improving your organization's ability to quickly segment and run different types of campaigns/reports using these fields.

- Blacklist Competitors –

Next, let's discuss blacklisting your competitors. The "Black Listed" field in Marketo is a special field that prevents any emails from being sent to leads who've been identified as those never to receive another email of any kind from your organization, even operation emails. An *operational* email is one that bypasses the unsubscribe option that a person may have due to opting out of marketing emails. If opts out of marketing communications, but then goes and voluntarily fills out a request for an eBook on your website, the Thank You email that's sent is an operational email, not a "Marketing" one promoting anything. If that person is blacklisted in Marketo, they will not receive any type of email, period!

To set up this type of campaign, create a new smart-campaign with the following logic:

Smart List Tab Criteria

(1) Filter - Member of Smart List = Competitors (**described in chapter 1**)

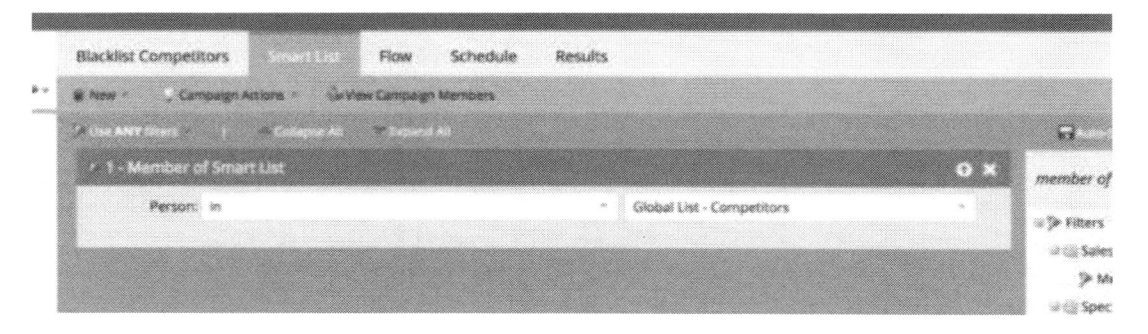

Flow Tab Criteria:

(1) Change Data Value on the "blacklisted" field to = True

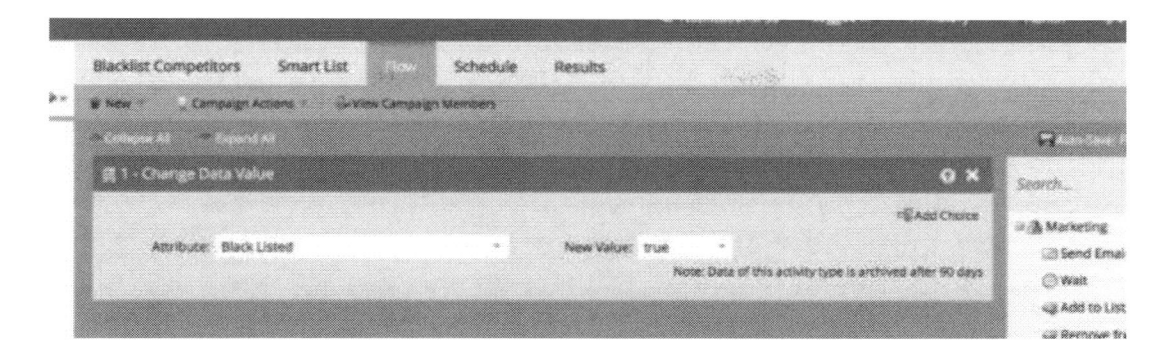

Schedule Tab Criteria:

Set this as a recurring batch campaign by selecting "**Schedule Recurrence**" to run nightly at 2am (or any late hour), preventing any interference with more important marketing campaigns scheduled to run during the day.

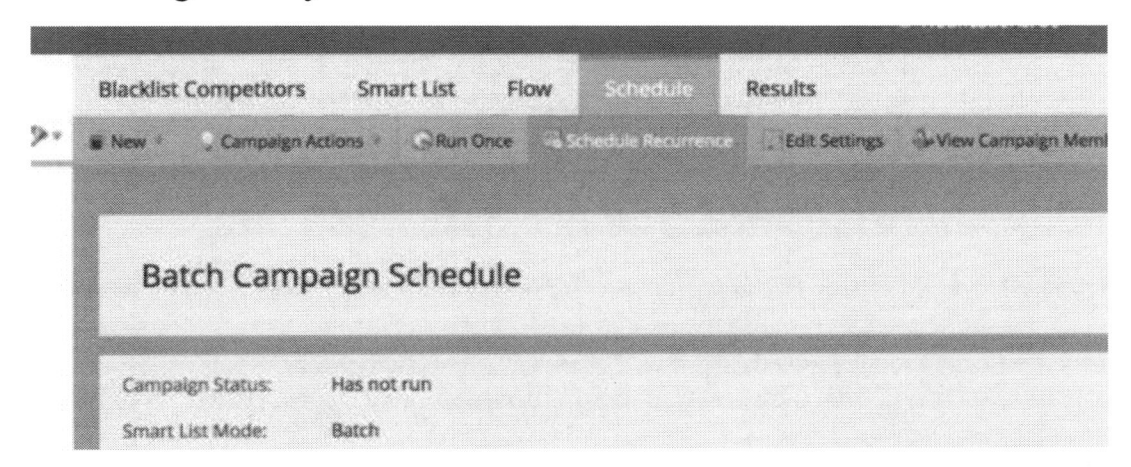

Now moving forward, if your competitors try downloading content on your website you at least have some form of precautions in place to increase the likelihood that some emails won't be sent to them. Sure, some may possibly get through but at least not the majority of them!

- **Email Invalid** –

Tracking email bounces can be tough for some customers and a complete nightmare for those whose sending domain gets blacklisted due to a huge volume of bounces. If you've been in the latter scenario, it's definitely time to cut down on the email blasts to randomly bought email addresses. But, for those who follow spam and privacy laws there are still times when an occasional email(s) bounces or an invalid email slips through the cracks and makes its way into CRM. This is exactly why it's highly recommended that the below three campaigns are created and scheduled to run nightly. Having these smart-campaigns will put your mind at ease knowing there's precautions in pace and allow you to focus on more important tasks at hand. Don't worry about bounce backs and let Marketo (the robot) track this for you!

You'll need three campaigns to accomplish a relatively air-tight email bounce-back system. One for hard-bounces, one for soft-bounces, and the third for resetting the email invalid field on any leads where their email is modified by an admin (typically to fix the reason emails sent to that address are bouncing).

Campaign 01 - Hard Bounce > Email Invalid

Smart List Tab Criteria

(1) Filter - Email Bounces = Any + (Add 2 Constraints for "Date of Activity" in past 90 days **AND** Min. Number of Times (that an email hard bounces) is = to 2)

- The reason for allowing 2 hard bounces prior to marking someone as email invalid is that by their very nature hard-bounces are a permanent failure with the email address. In some cases, if the email hard bounces after the 1st time, there's a small likelihood it may send after the 2nd try, but if it fails after the 2nd attempt it will most likely never repair itself. Setting it to 2 times will give those few another chance.

(2) Filter - Email Invalid = False - (the purpose of this filter is to exclude those who have already been marked as Email Invalid = True from unnecessarily re-entering the campaign)

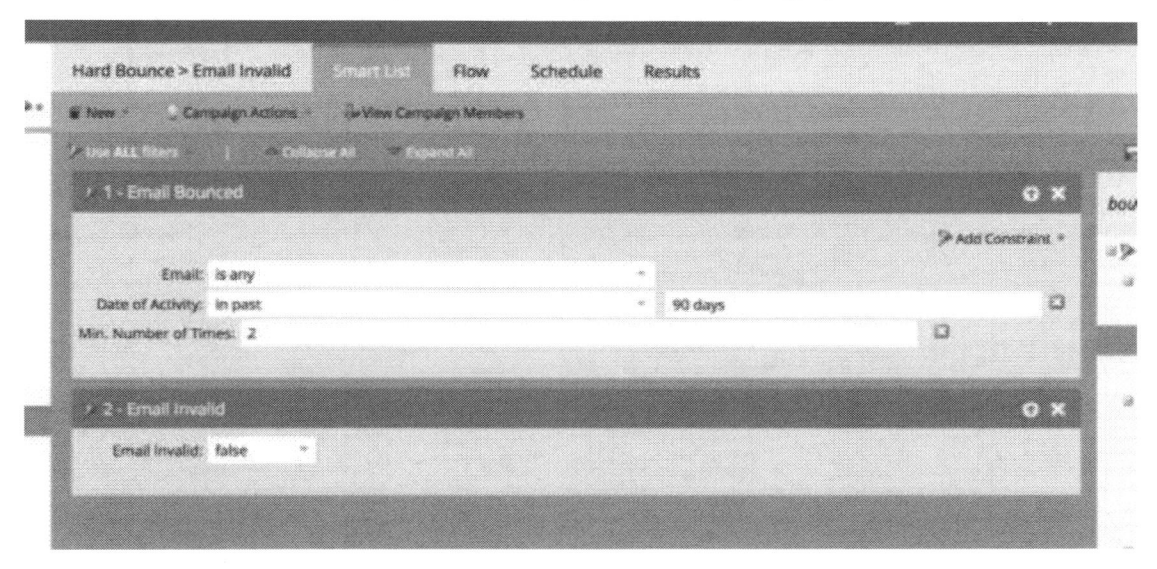

Flow Tab Criteria:

(1) Change Data Value - Email invalid = True

(2) Change Data Value - Email invalid Cause = "**Email Hard Bounced 2nd Time - {{system.dateTime}}**"

- The reason for the {{system.dateTime}} token will stamp the exact

system date & time the 2nd email hard bounced. To view each bounce date & time, refer to that lead's activity log.

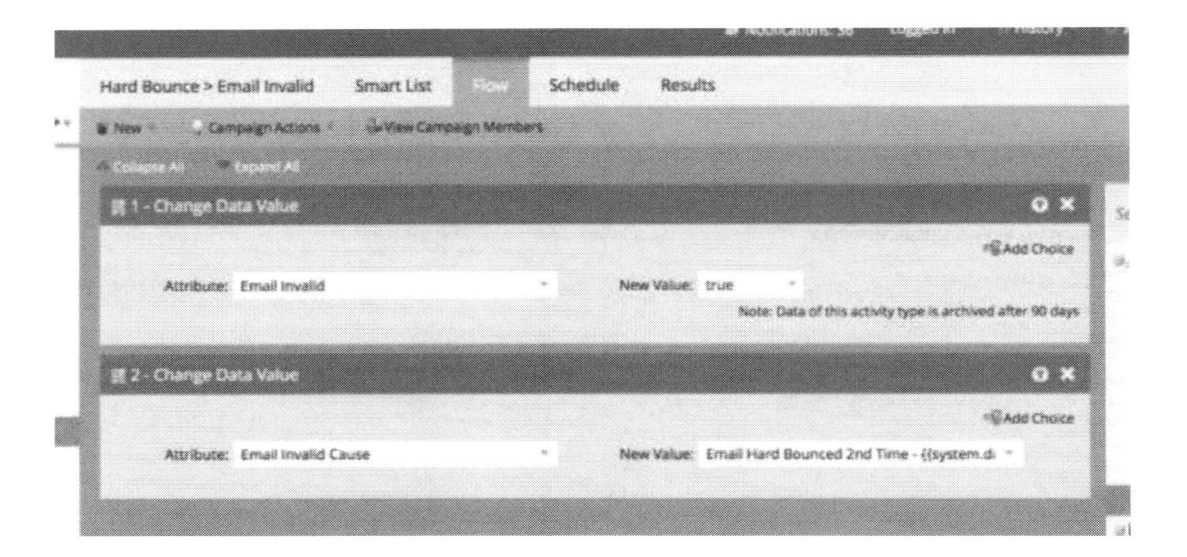

Schedule Tab Criteria:

Towards the center of the schedule tab, set the setting to allow "**Each person can run through this flow every time**". This will allow Marketo to process email bounces up to 2 times before marking someone as email invalid = True. Set this as a recurring batch campaign by selecting "**Schedule Recurrence**" to run nightly at 2am (or any late hour), preventing any interference with more important marketing campaigns scheduled to run during the day. Using a trigger in this campaign may bog down your instance during large email sends as leads will progress through this campaign if their email bounce in real-time, potentially impacting other marketing campaigns running during the day.

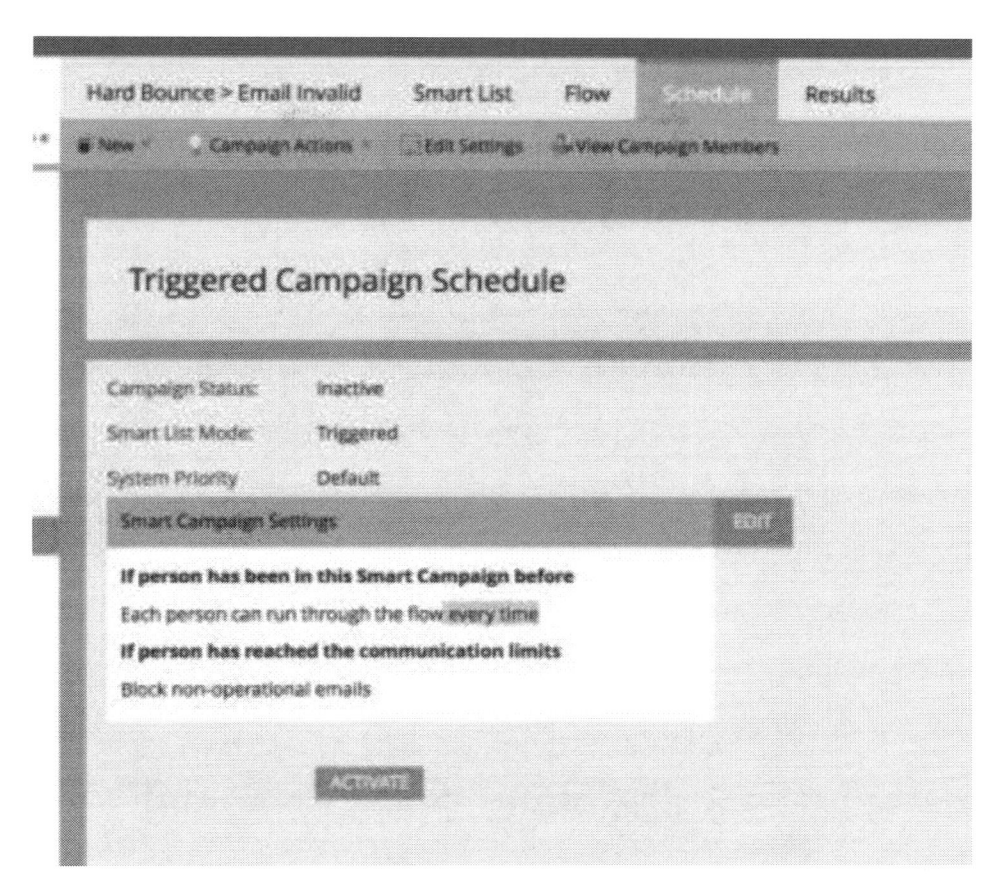

[Screenshot: Triggered Campaign Schedule page showing Campaign Status: Inactive, Smart List Mode: Triggered, System Priority: Default, and Smart Campaign Settings: "If person has been in this Smart Campaign before — Each person can run through the flow every time", "If person has reached the communication limits — Block non-operational emails", with an ACTIVATE button.]

Next and to save time, you'll want to *clone* this campaign and rename it for "**Soft Bounce > Email Invalid**". The campaign structure is similar but does have some changes that will be required. To clone, right click on the campaign and select "Clone", as shown below:

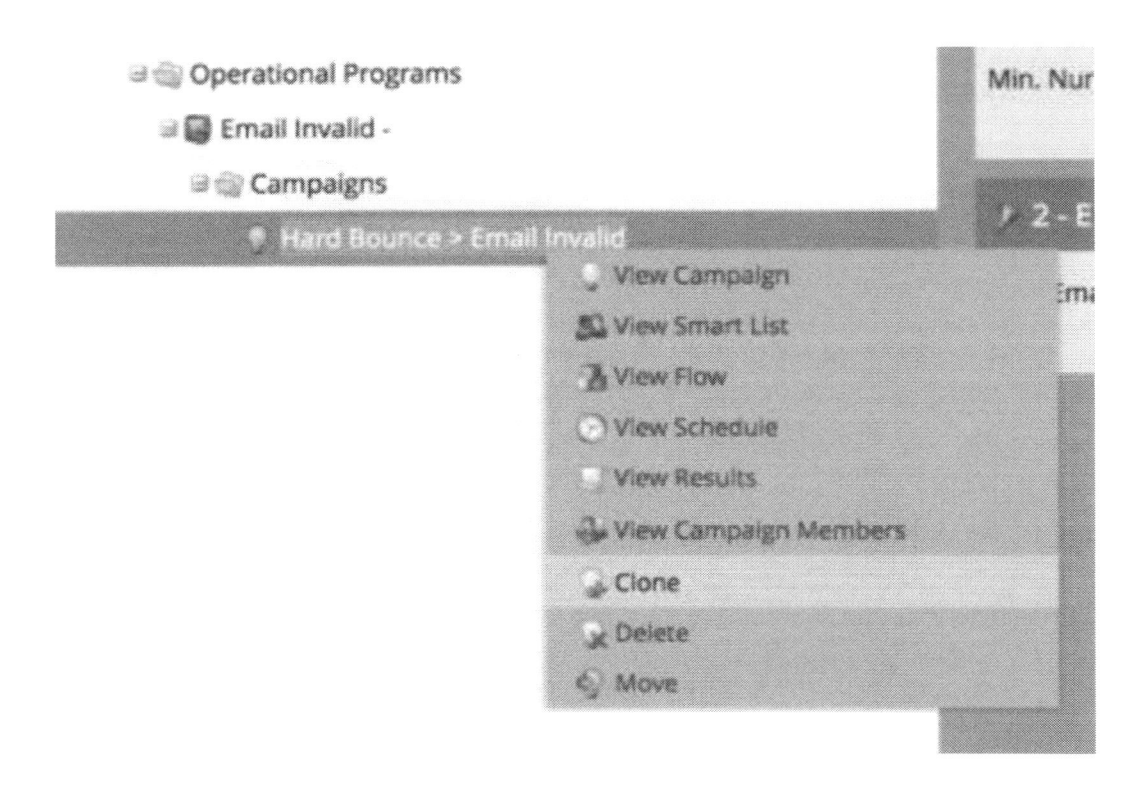

Campaign 02 - Soft Bounce > Email Invalid

Filter - Email <u>Soft</u> Bounces = Any + (Add 2 Constraints for "Date of Activity" in past 90 days **AND** Min. Number of Times (that an email hard bounces) is = to <u>3</u>)

- The reason for allowing 3 soft bounces prior to marking someone as email invalid is that by their very nature soft-bounces are a temporary failure with the email address.

    In most cases, if the email hard bounces after the 1st time, there's a high likelihood it will repair itself and send

    after the 2nd try. Giving it an extra chance to resolve itself

    is recommended. But if it fails after the 3rd attempt it will most likely not repair resolve itself.

Filter - Email Invalid = False - (the purpose of this filter is to exclude those who have already been marked as Email Invalid = True from unnecessarily re-entering the campaign)

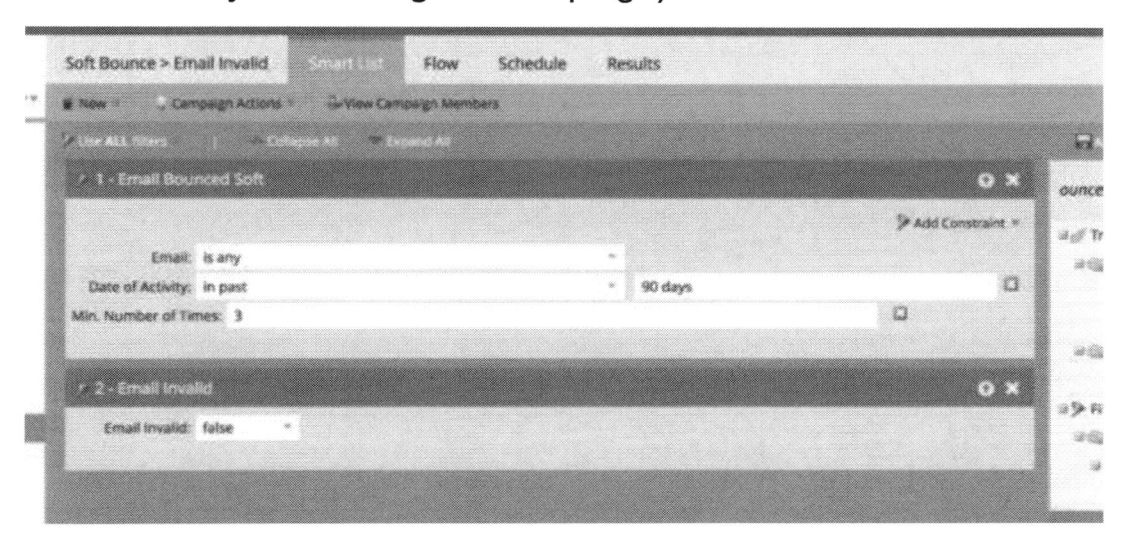

Flow Tab Criteria:

(1) Change Data Value - Email invalid = True
(2) Change Data Value - Email invalid Cause = "**Email Soft Bounced 3rd Time - {{system.dateTime}}**"

- The reason for the {{system.dateTime}} token will stamp the exact system date & time the 3rd email soft bounced. To view each bounce date & time, refer to that lead's activity log.

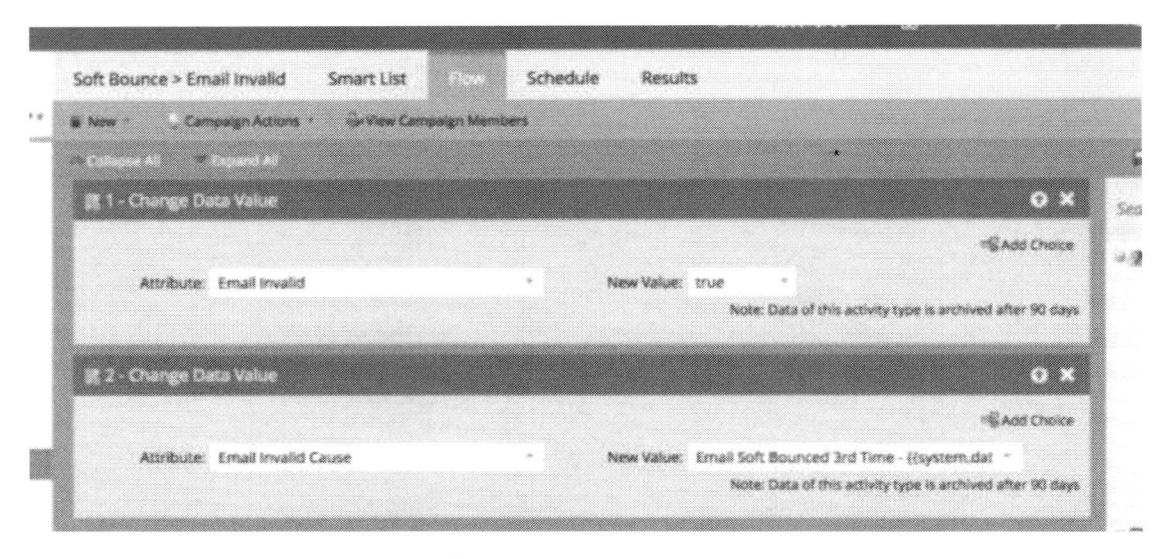

Schedule Tab Criteria:

Towards the center of the schedule tab, set the setting to allow **"Each person can run through this flow every time"**. This will allow Marketo to process email bounces up to 3 times before marking someone as email invalid = True. Set this as a recurring batch campaign by selecting **"Schedule Recurrence"** to run nightly at 2am (or any late hour), preventing any interference with more important marketing campaigns scheduled to run during the day. Using a trigger in this campaign may bog down your instance during large email sends as leads will progress through this campaign if their email bounce in real-time, potentially impacting other marketing campaigns running during the day.

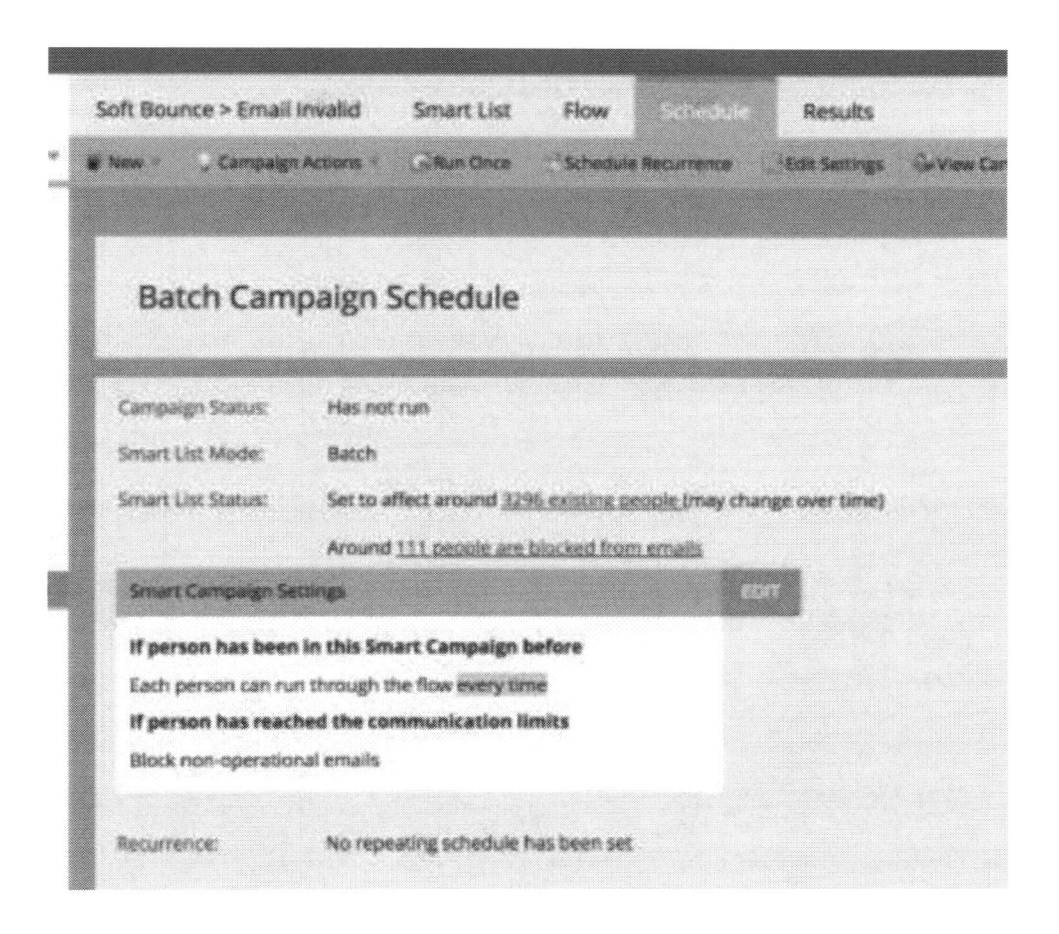

The 3rd and final campaign is for situations where a lead is marked as email invalid already and a Marketo admin goes into their lead-record to edit the email address after the fact. This campaign will detect that change and revert the lead's email-invalid back to "False", assuming the admin is making a change to their email to resolve the bounce issue. If they enter an incorrect email again, it isn't concerning as that lead will bounce 2 or 3 more times and be marked as email invalid again.

Name this 3rd campaign "**Reset Email Invalid**" and set it up using the following logic:

Campaign 03 - Reset Email Invalid

Smart List Tab Criteria

(1) Trigger - Data Value Changes - On the "**Email Address**" field.

(2) Filter - Email Invalid = True

- The logic here states that if Marketo detects any change on the email address field for any lead the currently has their email invalid field set to True, they will proceed to the flow tab.

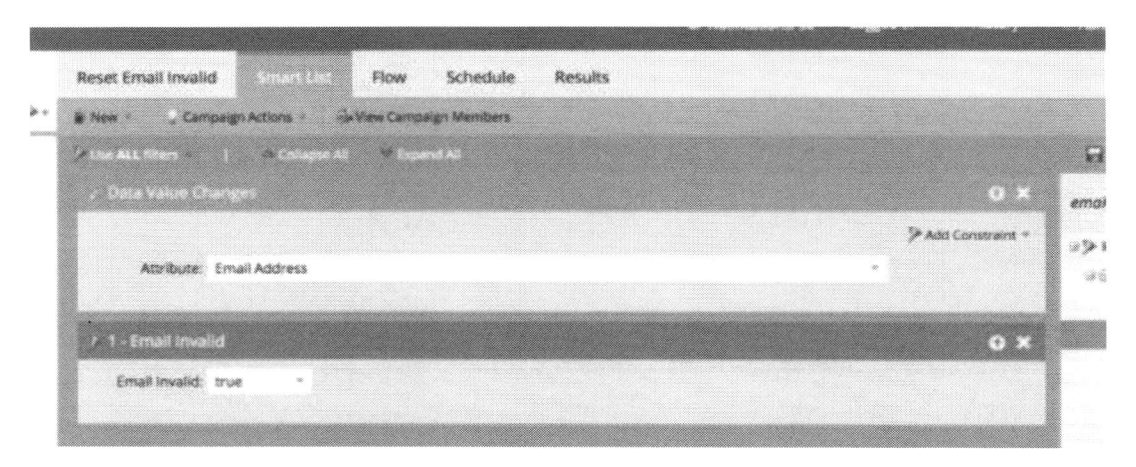

Flow Tab Criteria:

(1) Change Data Value - of "Email Invalid" to = False
(2) Change Data Value - of "Email Invalid Reason" to = "Null"

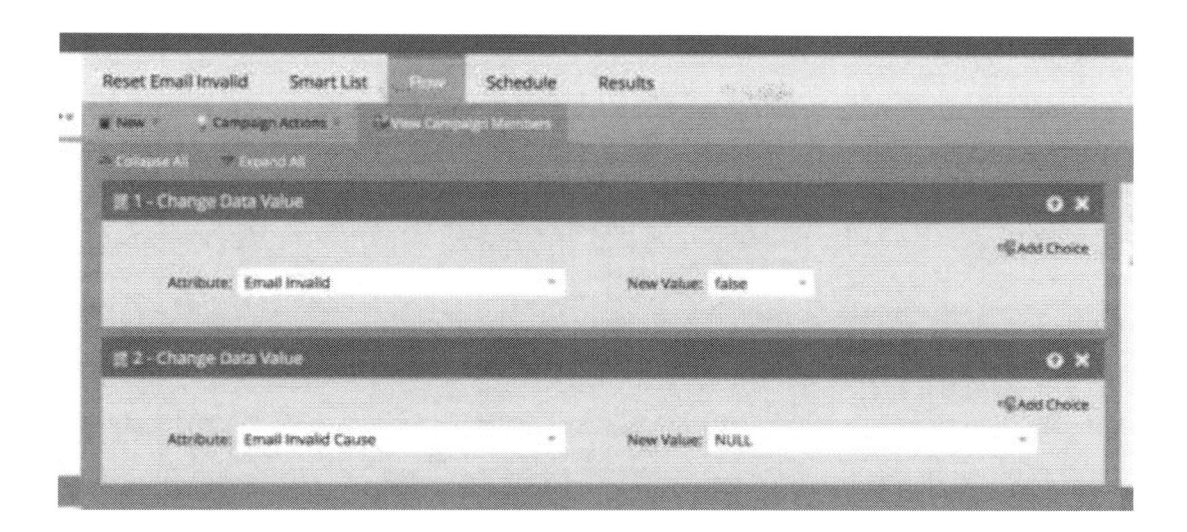

Schedule Tab Criteria:

Towards the center of the schedule tab, set the setting to allow **"Each person can run through this flow every time"**. This will allow Marketo to process leads who have been tagged as Email Invalid = True in this campaign every time their email is corrected. Since this campaign has a trigger in it you will simply need to click "Activate" toward the bottom of the screen to enable the smart-campaign.

Triggered Campaign Schedule

Campaign Status: Inactive
Smart List Mode: Triggered
System Priority: Default

Smart Campaign Settings

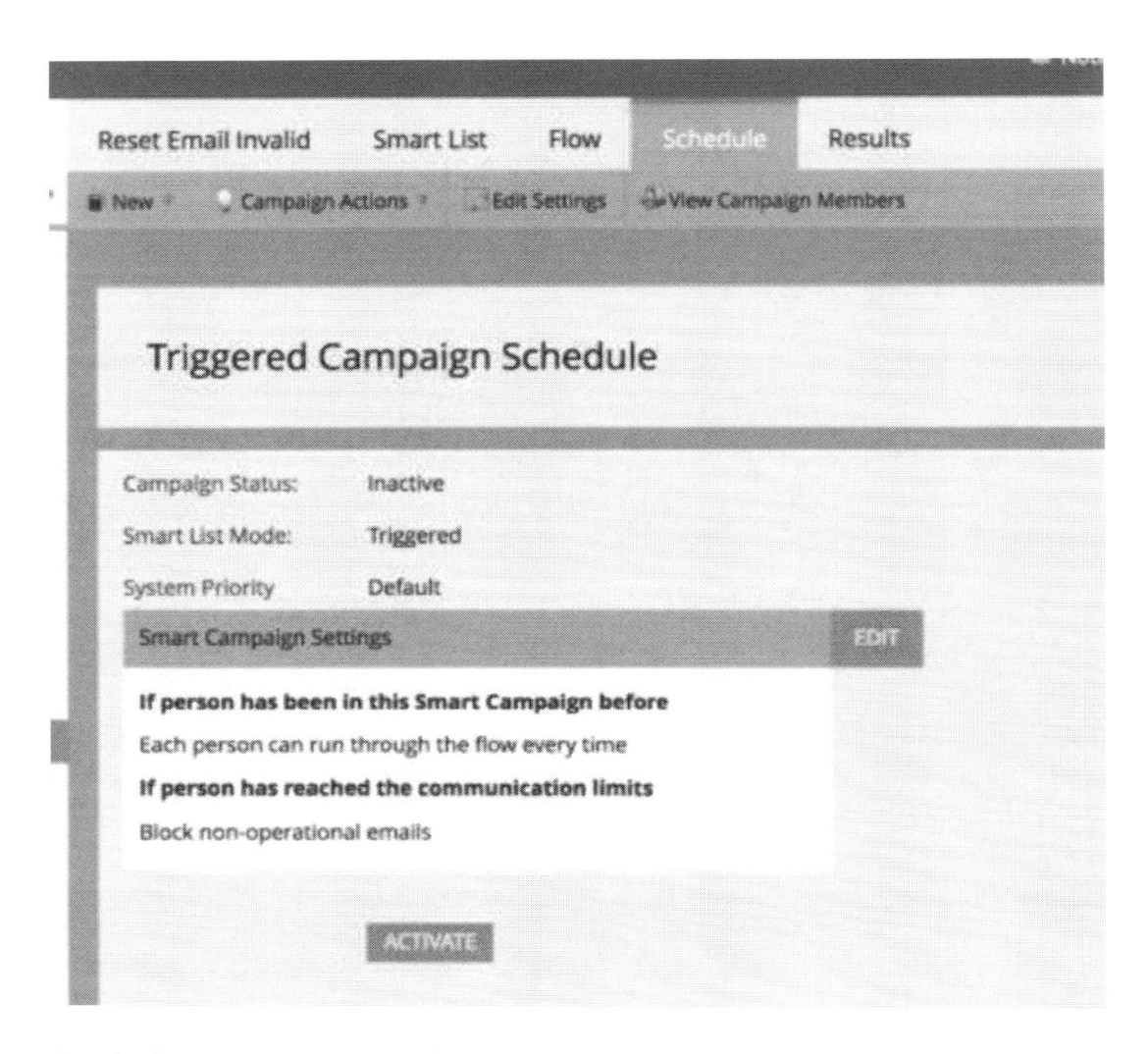

If person has been in this Smart Campaign before
Each person can run through the flow every time

If person has reached the communication limits
Block non-operational emails

Again just as a recap, what this campaign is doing is ensuring that if a record has their email invalid field set to True, and Marketo detects someone going into the system and making a Data Value change to the email address field, regardless if it's correct or not, Marketo will assume the person going in is attempting to fix the email address field for that record. It will automatically change the email invalid field back to False and null out any reason captured. In the event the person makes an incorrect edit to the email address, it's nothing to worry about. That record will flow through either of the first two campaigns and be marked as email invalid again. No harm is done and at least your Marketo instance has a way to ensure no records are chronically bouncing with every subsequent send.

- Retroactively Stamp Acquisition Program Field on CRM records –

For those who have a brand new Marketo instance provisioned and are connecting with a CRM, it's important to keep any source and acquisition fields updated so person source metrics are not skewed. Once you've connected Marketo with a CRM, there will be a period where all person records (leads & contacts) will sync. Since the "**Acquisition Program**" field is a Marketo-specific field, these records will not have a value when they enter Marketo. Below, is a best-practice operational program with a single campaign that will stamp a value to the "Acquisition Program" field for all leads/contacts that go through the initial sync to indicate they were not acquired through any program, but rather were sourced prior to syncing into Marketo. This will prevent your metrics and reporting from attributing unnecessary credit to programs that in-fact did not actually source those leads.

This type of operational campaign should be set up or ran right after the initial sync before any leads have a chance to interact with any other marketing programs or forms. Otherwise those lead records will have an incorrect value stamped onto that field as soon as they interact with their first form that's local to a Marketo program. This can skew your reporting and be a headache to retroactively fix.

Below is the recommended campaign structure to build this one-time campaign. If you are creating this type of operational campaign after your marketing programs are in full swing, for example if you've just inherited an instance and realized this is missing, you'll need to work backward to correct your acquisition values on those records. You'll need to reference and become very comfortable with reviewing individual lead activity logs and It's highly recommended to work with a Marketo consultant for the best and easiest path forward.

Smart List Tab Criteria

(1) Filter: Person was Created and add (constraint = Source) and that equals "salesforce.com" (as an example) – If MS Dynamics or another CRM is connected, use the different value accordingly.

(2) Filter: "Acquisition Program" field = is empty

- The logic here states that as soon as Marketo detects leads created, and they came from Salesforce, and if their current acquisition program fields is empty (which it would be since they just came into the database), they will then proceed into the follow tab.

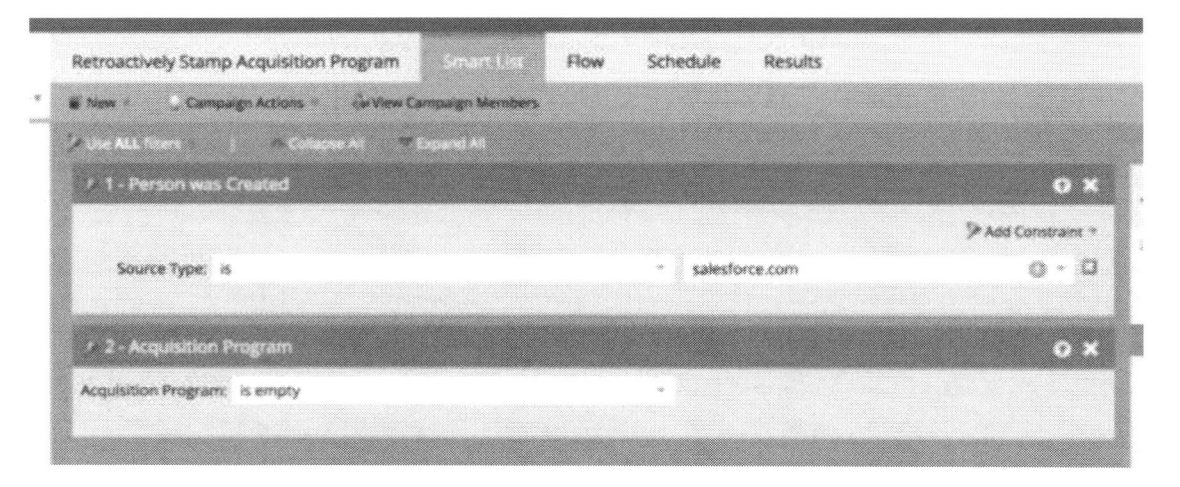

Flow Tab Criteria:

(1) Change Data Value - on the "**Acquisition Program**" field to = "Synced from CRM" (or something similar)

(2) Change Data Value - on the "**Source**" field to have an "Add Choice". The rule is if "Source" = is empty, then change to a new value of = "Synced from CRM" (otherwise set "do nothing" in the default choice in the event the source field is populated from CRM

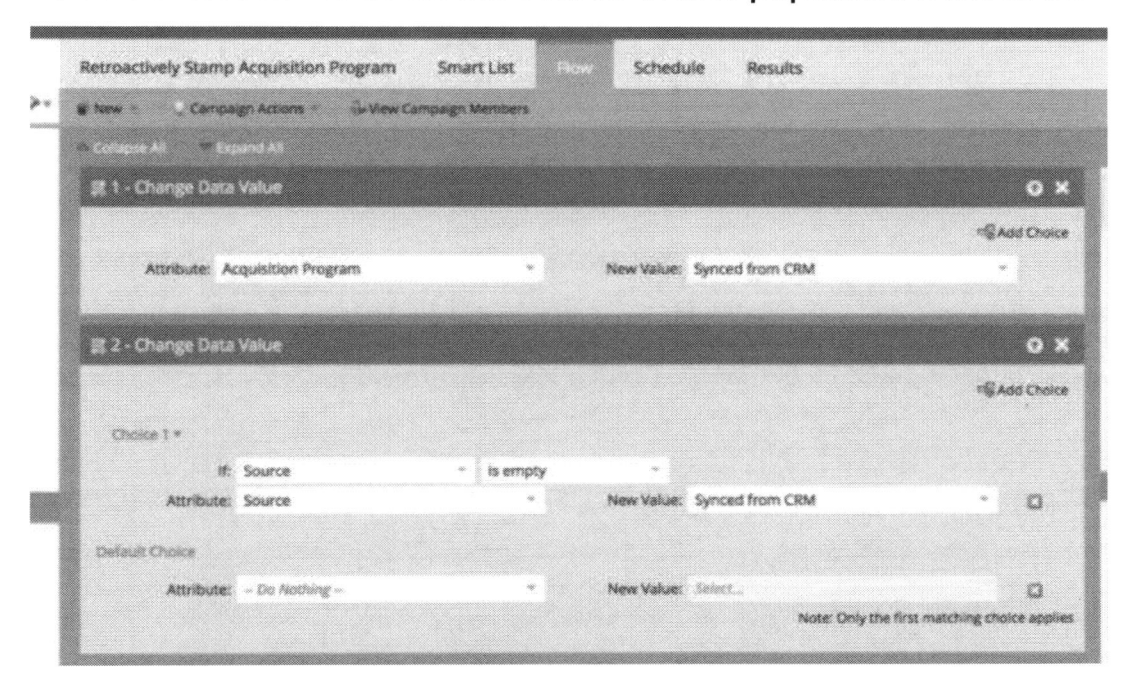

Schedule Tab Criteria:

Towards the center of the schedule tab, set the setting to allow **"Each person can run through this flow once"**. Set this as a recurring batch campaign by selecting **"Schedule Recurrence"** to run nightly at 2am (or any late hour), preventing any interference with more important marketing campaigns scheduled to run during the day. This way, there is a fail-safe campaign to ensure that all net-new leads and contacts originating out of salesforce have their true source populated at all times as they sync into Marketo

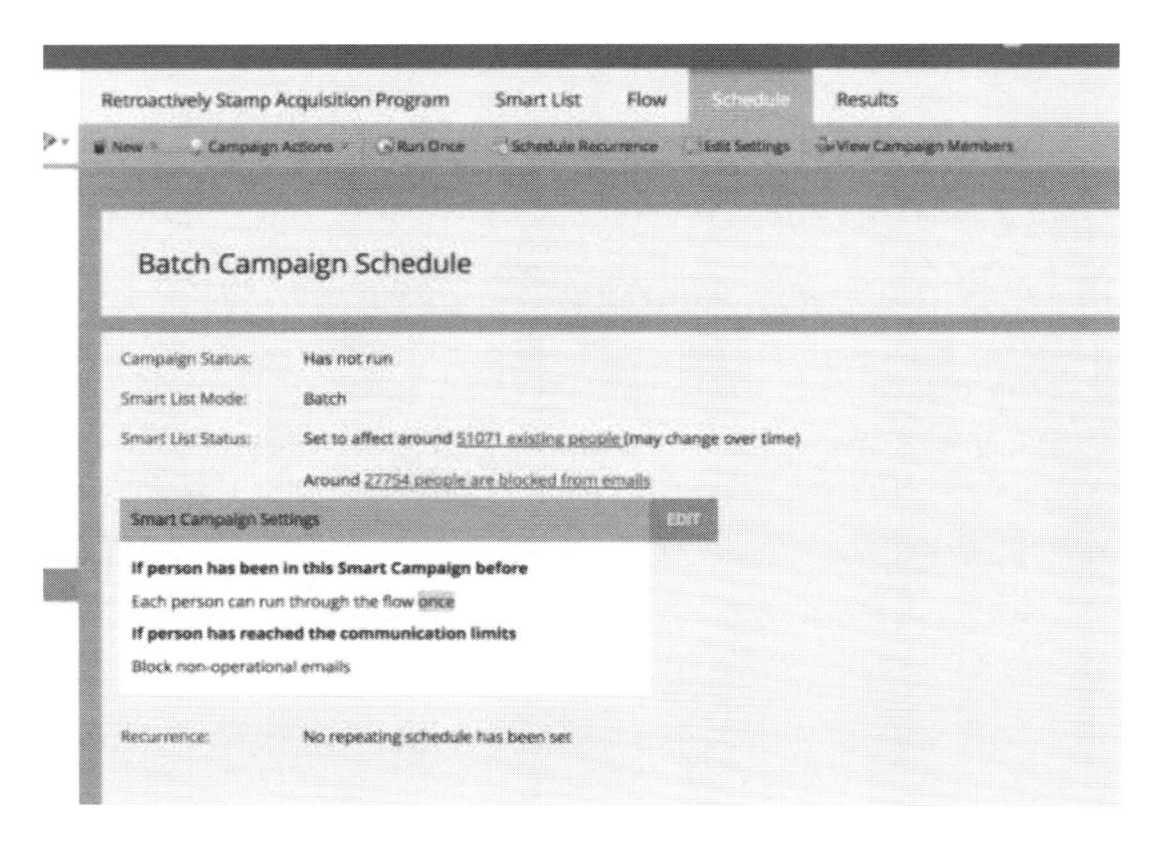

[Screenshot of Batch Campaign Schedule interface]

Having the above campaign in place, your organization will be set up for success whether you current are or will eventually use Marketo's Revenue Cycle Explorer for **first-touch** attribution reporting.

- List Import Program –

Next, we'll discuss the inevitable scenario of importing lead records into Marketo via a CSV or excel file. All organizations will do this for different purposes but not all follow the same best practice. What tends to happen is there will be a need at one point or another in the maturity curve of any organization to buy a list of leads to market to. Some lists are more targeted than others but in almost all cases what occurs is that list is simply uploaded into Marketo's database section external to any Marketo program.

To reiterate, this should **NOT** happen, and every organization should do it's best to avoid blindly going into Marketo's database section and selecting "Import List", as shown below:

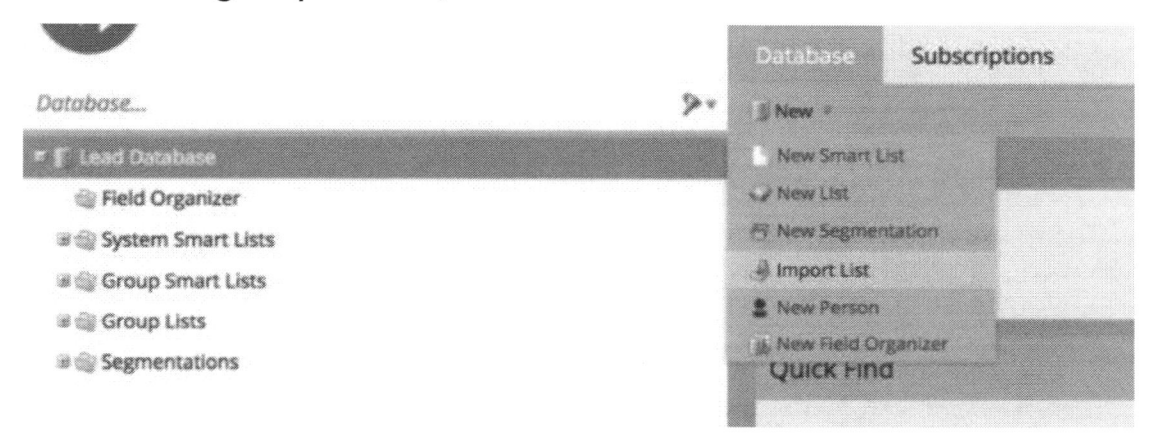

The reason to avoid this is simple. When you import leads using the above section into Marketo, all of the people on your CSV will go into Marketo as desired but their acquisition and source fields will be blank (since they didn't enter Marketo by submitting their information via a form). Next, those same leads that were sourced through a list-purchase receive an email, click a link, land on a landing page with a form for a gated asset or event registration on it, and once submitted their "Acquisition Program" field and potential their source fields will be incorrectly populated.

As described earlier in this chapter, Marketo will stamp the acquisition of any lead upon its first form submission (if their acquisition program field is empty at the time, which imported leads would have). Fast forward a few weeks and your acquisition metrics are skewed and reporting is not accurate. Leave unmanaged for an extended amount of time and your first-touch attribution metrics will be completely useless.

The best practice to account for this scenario is to create a simple "List Import" program template. By creating a "template", you are creating a program for the purpose of cloning every time you will be importing a list of net-new purchased leads. Please note that this is NOT for importing leads from an event such as a tradeshow. Lists of leads from events should be imported to their specific event programs to stamp the acquisition of those leads from that specific event. This "List Import" program is meant to isolate your imported leads from other marketing program analytics.

To illustrate, let's create a program and associate it to the "List Import" channel. If there is no separate "List Import" channel in your instance, create one to separate this channel from other marketing channels. Once you create the program, click on the "Members" tab at the top and select the "Import Members" tab:

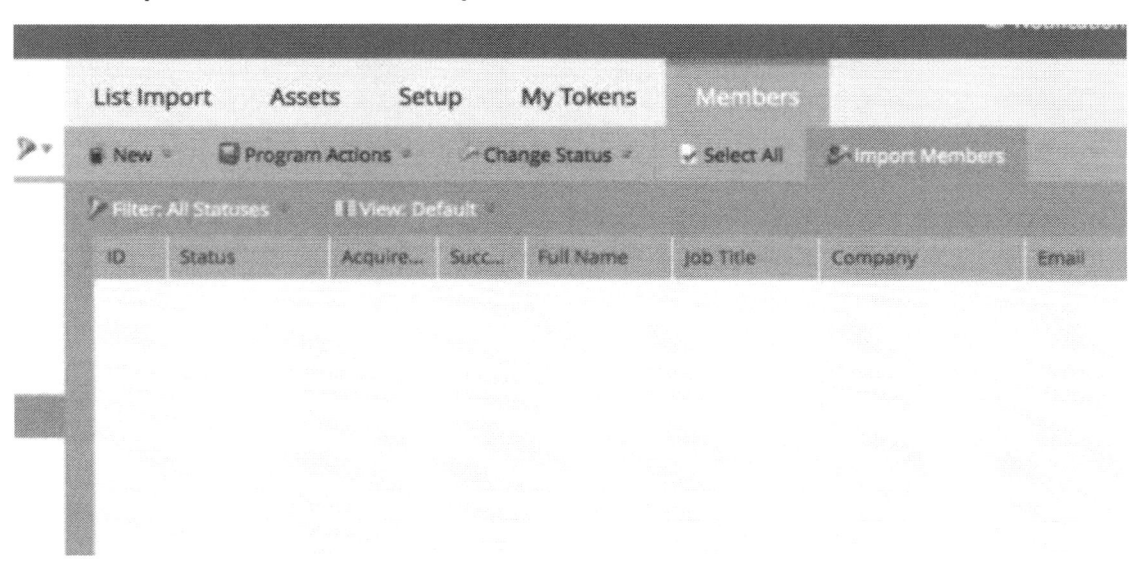

When the CSV of lead records is imported, their acquisition program will be easily set to the list import program you've cloned. For example, the next time a new list is purchased from a vendor named "Vendor ABC", you can:

(1) Right-click on this "List Import" program template and select "Clone"
(2) Name the new program "LI-YYYY-MM-DD-VendorABC List", or something similar"
(3) When created, select "Members" tab and click "Import Members".
(4) Follow on-screen instructions to import your list

Now, when you view your program performance reports, you'll easily be able to compare which marketing programs are accurately sourcing and contributing net-new leads to your organization without mixing the analytics with purchased leads.

Again, this should only be considered for purchased leads and not ALL list imports. Those lists belonging to marketing programs or events should be uploading into their respective Marketo programs (using the same methodology above).

- Data Management & Segmentations -

Within Marketo, there are several different methods for how to manage data. We discussed a few of them in the above sections such as normalizing fields, suppressing certain types of people, and ensuring no email addresses are chronically bouncing.

Another popular way to manage and filter data in Marketo is through the use of a smart-list. What's most attractive about smart-lists is how easy they filter the correct grouping of people needed to include in any campaign (using the "Member of smart-list" filter).

By its very nature, a smart-list itself is constantly turned on and scanning the database to find matches of records to the filter-criteria you've used in them. When I say constant, I mean it will do it again and again, even if it just queried the database a few seconds ago. This constant querying isn't usually an issue when you have a relatively manageable size of smart lists in Marketo. But, all too often it's easy to get carried away!

What I've noticed is that many marketing ops teams create a simple smart list to include in a smart campaign, and once the campaign has run, they don't delete it or re-use it. Fast forward this habit 6 months or a year later and your instance can turn into a cluttered nightmare with smart-lists that are constantly querying the database every second of the day. Compound this issue with more complex smart-lists that have five to ten, or even more filters inside of them and the querying gets much more complex. What will occur eventually is Marketo will get bogged down and your entire instance will start experiencing performance issues that will make using Marketo painfully slow and resemble an application that may have used dial-up internet in the early '90s. Not fun at all.

It's also important to understand that avoiding the use of smart-lists is not practical. They are core to Marketo and should be leveraged when needed. The key take-away is to emphasize being aware of how these smart-lists function and keeping in mind the importance of reusing in other smart campaigns when possible. Delete them after they've been used when you know they most likely will never be needed again. This way, you aren't adding a lag to the overall performance.

A best practice that is recommended is to leverage Marketo's segmentations located in the **database**. These are great because they allow you to call on segmented leads anytime without using smart lists. They can be leveraged as regular triggers and filters individually inside of smart-campaigns (instead of a smart-list), and they do not query the system every second of the day alleviating the aforementioned problems lots of companies run into.

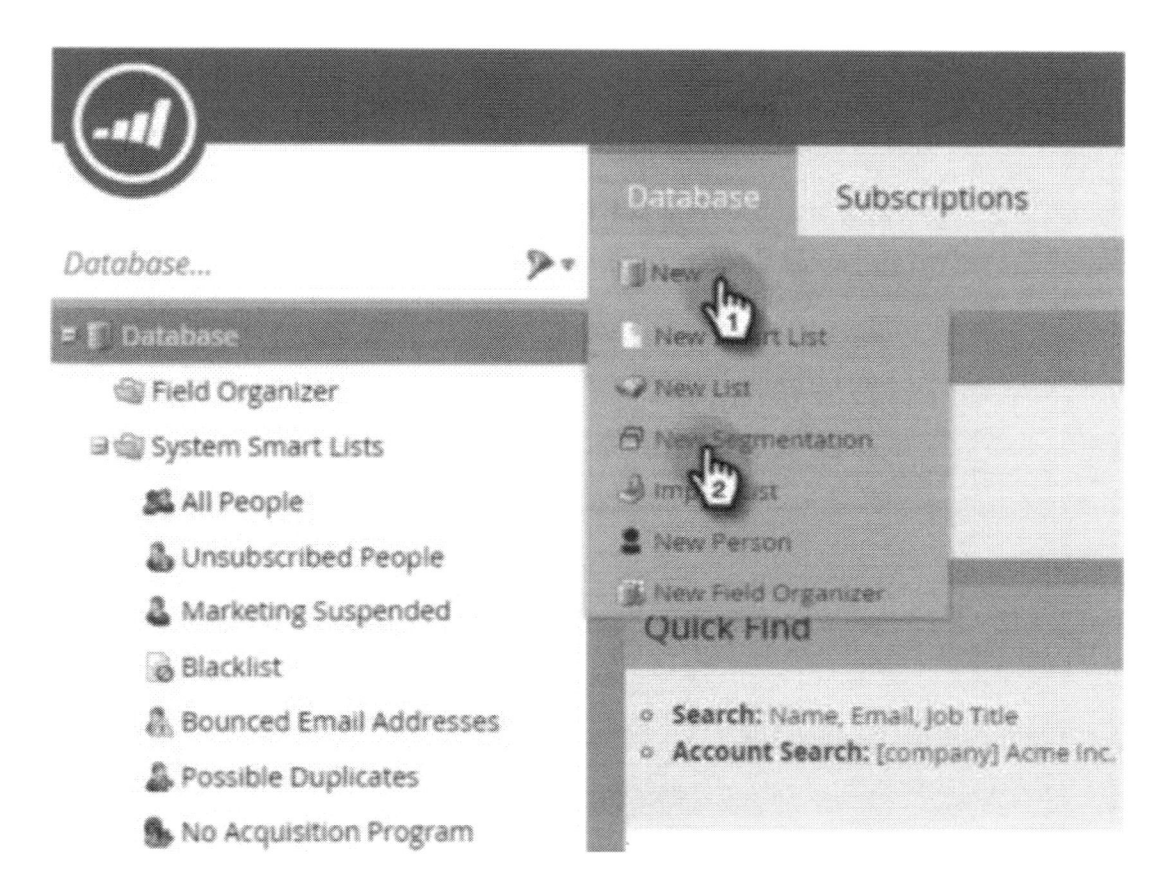

When setting up a segmentation strategy, keep in mind that you can have up to only 20 segmentations in Marketo and each segmentation can have up to 100 segments in it. That's 2000 segments total! I have yet run into a Marketo customer that has used up all of their 20 allocated slots and are actually using all of them for marketing.

How you and your team should think about creating Segmentations is that they need to be geared toward your organization's Core segments that you **foresee using on a regular basis**. Think about the way you market to leads. What criteria come to mind immediately based on your organization' s ideal customer profile? You may want to group leads by product interest, by services line, by region, or all of the above. Let's create an example segmentation based on people from different geographical territories.

(1) Right click on the "**Segmentations**" folder and select "**New Segmentation**":

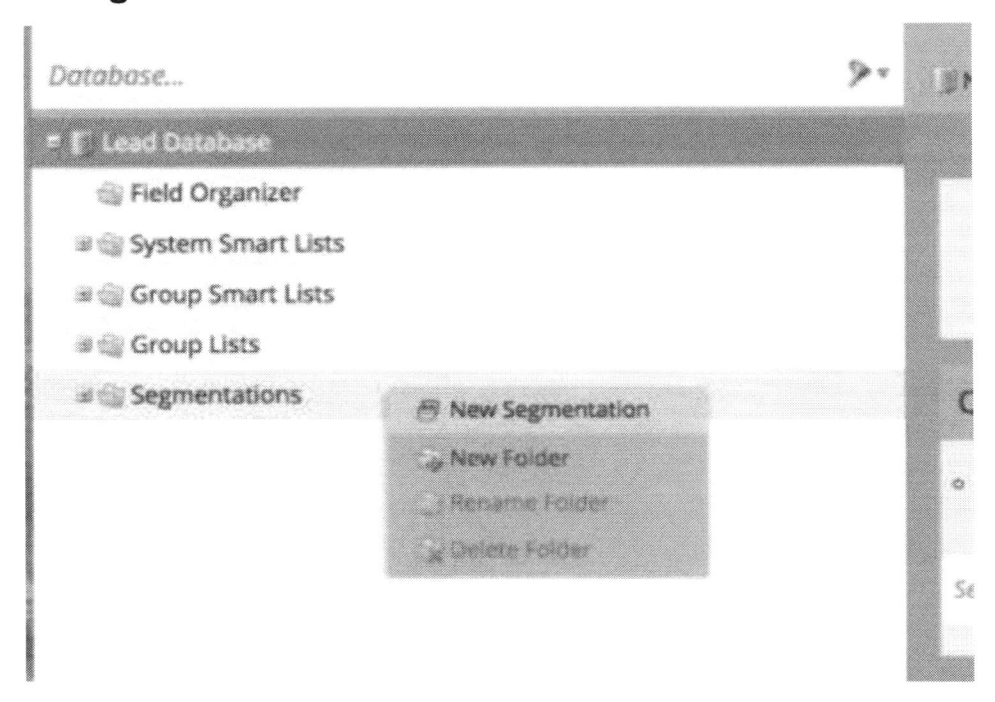

(2) Title it "**Geographical**"

(3) Once created, it will automatically create a "Default" segment by Marketo. This is mandatory and is simply used as a bucket for leads and contacts if they do not match any of the other specific segments you create.

(4) Click on "Add Segments" and add additional segments that are relevant to your territories and how leads are segmented for your organization. (Again, this is just an example and can be used for any fields that help segment your leads)

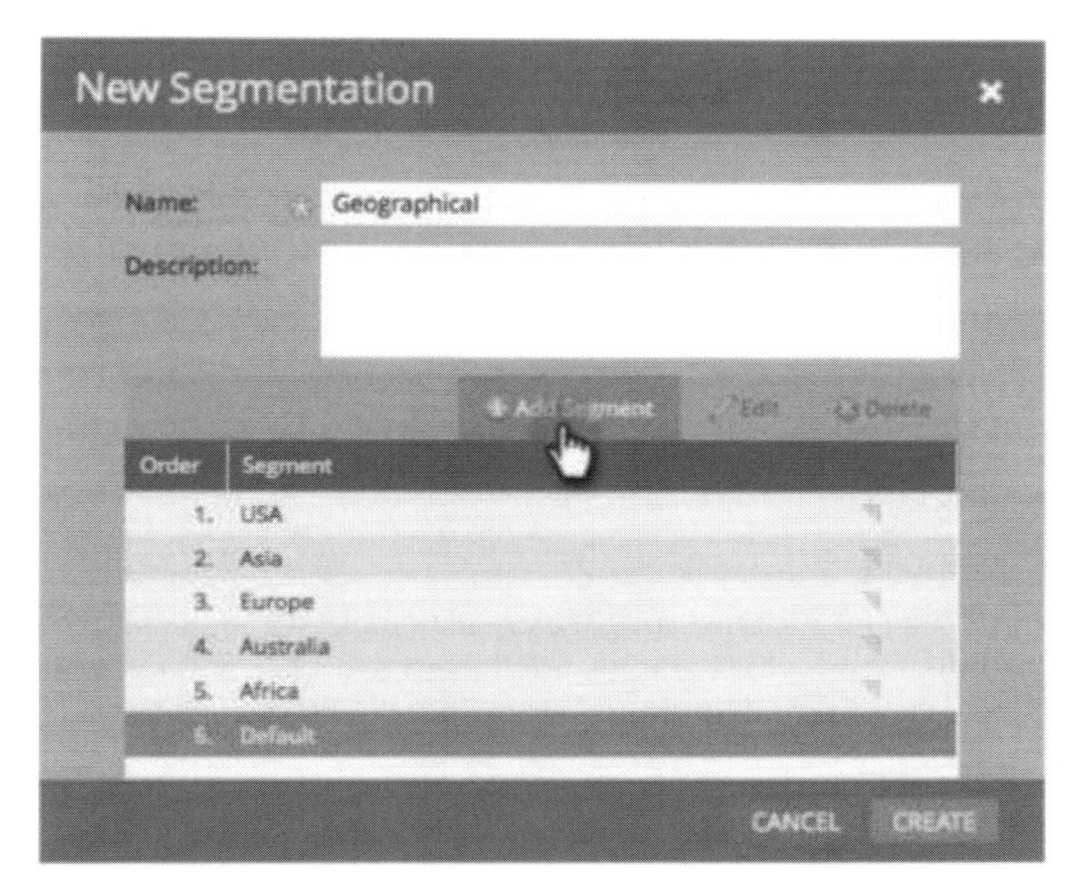

(5) The order of which you add segments is important. For example, Marketo immediately detects once a new lead enters the system and will start from the top-most segment and work its way down until that leads is assigned to the first segment that it matches to. It's important to understand that Marketo will assign any net-new person to the first segment they match, regardless if they could have matched others that are lower.

   a. An example of where this can come into play is for organizations with multiple product lines. This can be tricky for companies who have different products and want to create a system to assign leads based on whether they have purchased or are interested in one of their products. If this use case fits your organization, the best way to go about this is to create the following segment structure:

i. Product A, Product B, & Product C

ii. Product A, Product B

iii. Product A, Product C

iv. Product B, Product C

v. Product A

vi. Product B

vii. Product C

    1. Marketo will start with the top segment to check if leads have purchased or shown interest in all 3 products first. Then if that lead doesn't accommodate the criteria or logic for the top segment (showing interest in all three products for example), it will work its way down to the 2-product tier(s), and if the lead/contact does not match those, it will be assigned to one of the single tiers toward the bottom.

(6) When actually creating the segments, they work similar to a smart list. You'll need to select filters that match the criteria of the segment you are building. Since the example we are using is using geographical territories, you'll probably want to bring in the country, region, state, or any similar field. Set the values to the corresponding name of the segment:

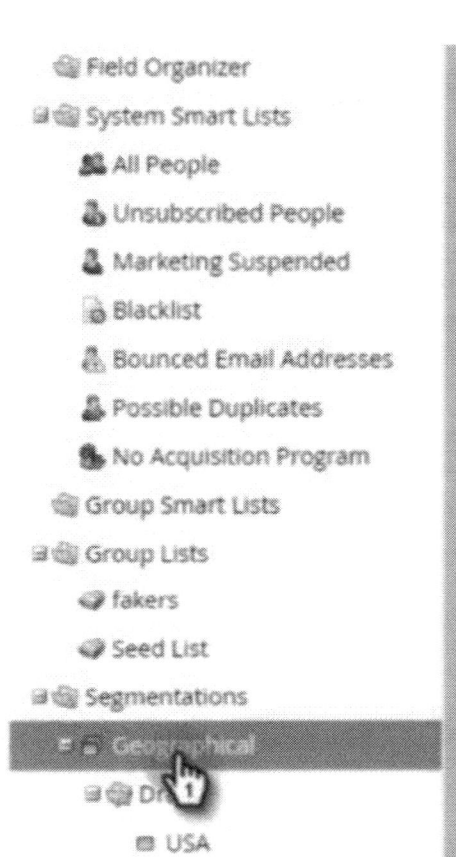

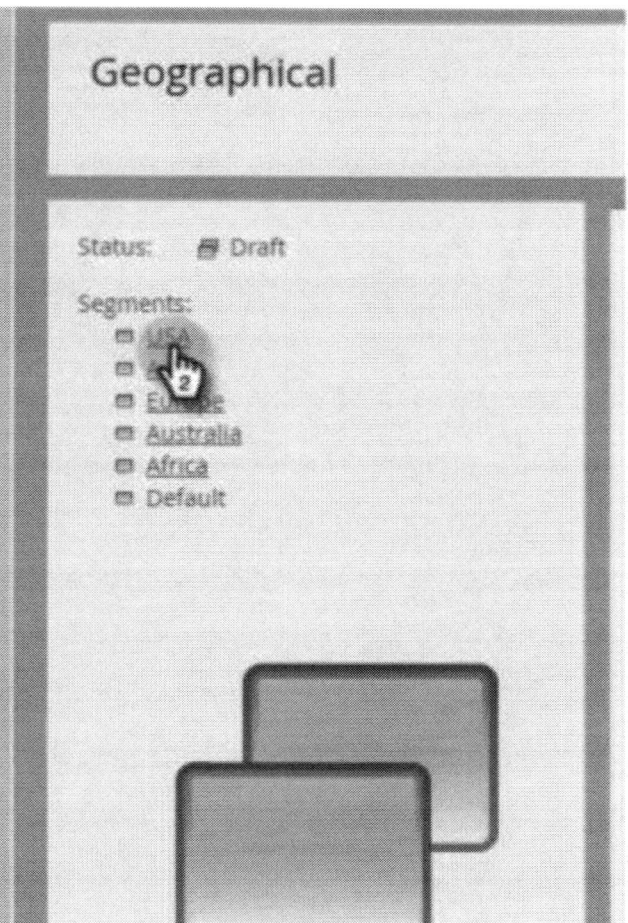

- Field Organizer
- System Smart Lists
  - All People
  - Unsubscribed People
  - Marketing Suspended
  - Blacklist
  - Bounced Email Addresses
  - Possible Duplicates
  - No Acquisition Program
- Group Smart Lists
- Group Lists
  - fakers
  - Seed List
- Segmentations
  - Geographical
    - Dr
      - USA
      - Asia
      - Europe

Geographical

Status: Draft

Segments:
- USA
- Asia
- Europe
- Australia
- Africa
- Default

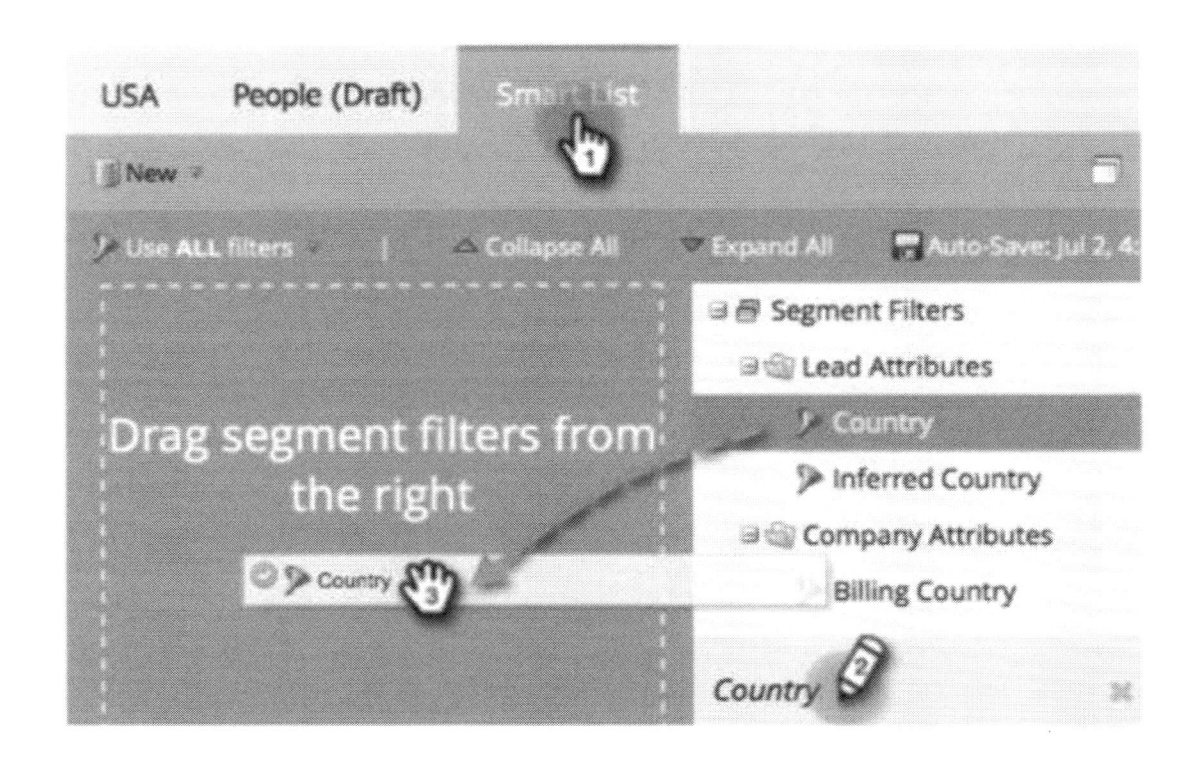

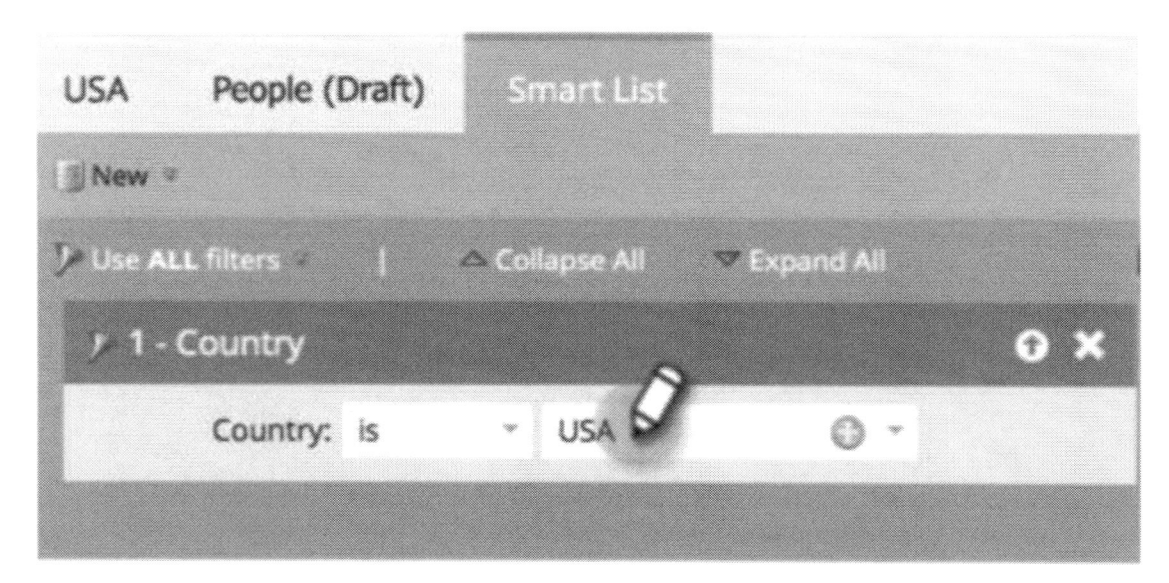

(7) **Repeat** the same steps for all of your segments

(8) Once completed, select "Segmentation Actions" toward the top tabs and select "Approve."

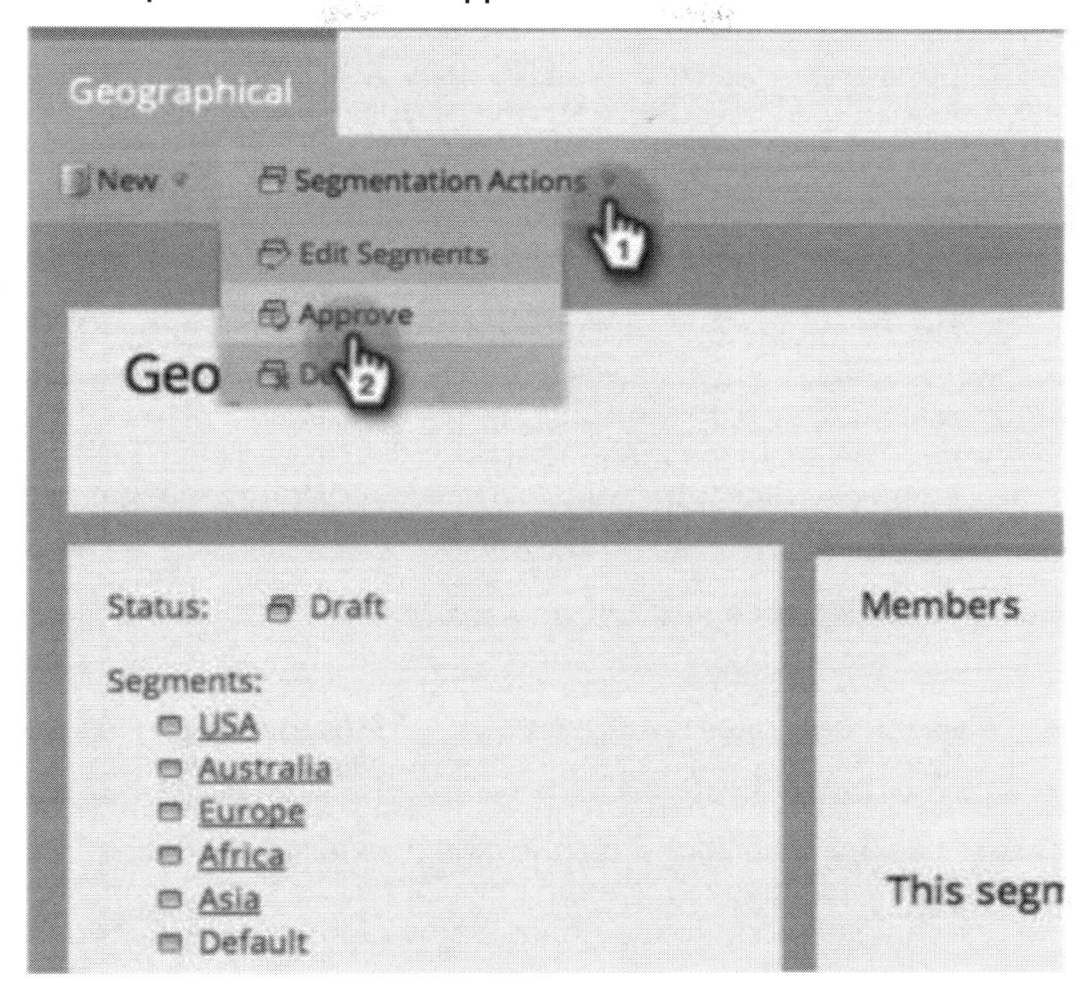

Once the segmentation is approved, you are now able to use the segments that have been built in different campaigns as filters and triggers, **without needing to build** a smart list every time. Now, one of the most useful ways to manage your current data and segment it within your campaigns is to apply Marketo's dynamic content.

-Dynamic Content-

The dynamic content feature in Marketo can be a huge time-saver! If you're hoping to give your prospects a more personalized touch, there is no need to create different assets like emails, landing pages, forms, etc., for each where you'll need to build complex workflows with logic such as "if you are in this specific geographical segment, send email one. If you are in another geographical segment, send email two."

Instead, you'll have the added benefit of building out a single email or landing page and displaying different content, images, forms, links and more to different leads based on the segment they belong to. This can make the difference between an efficient marketing team who leverages Marketo's automations successfully to one that may simply not be aware and is wasting time building separate assets from scratch to accommodate different segmented leads/contacts. Even though most may be on the right track in terms or improving engagement via personalization, those who do this manually will have an uphill tedious experience.

Let's walk through one **example using a landing page**. It's also worth noting that dynamic content only applies to emails, landing pages and snippets. It does not apply to forms *themselves* although you can use multiple forms on the same landing page based on who's viewing the page (for example different global regions may have different language forms on the same landing page depending on who is viewing it). Same applies to images and files in Marketo.

Applying Dynamic Content in Assets

Open any landing page and **select any editable area**, such as an image or any text. Editable areas in emails, landing pages, and snippets are very important for dynamic content to work. The more editable areas that are present in any asset, the more dynamic content you can apply, and in turn the more flexible each asset is to customize individually for any segment of leads you would like to target.

(1) Right click on the editable area and select "**Segment By**"

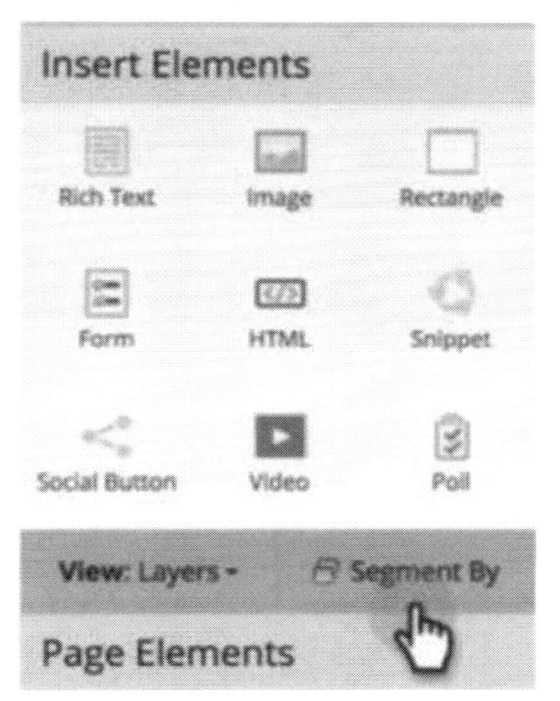

(2) A popup will appear asking which segmentation you would like to use. The below example shows a different segmentation that can be used based on either prospects or customers viewing the landing page:

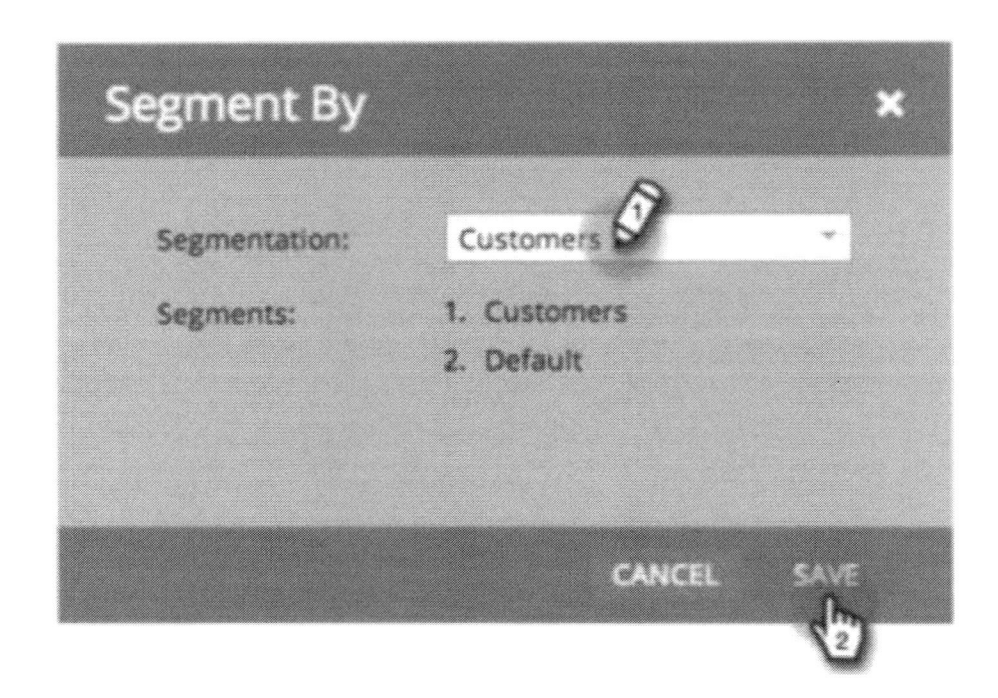

(3) Now, you will notice that the editable area you clicked on (image/text area/etc.) turned yellow briefly. This means that any prior content that was in that editable area as it appeared once you applied it to a segmentation is now applied to the ***default*** segment. If any leads belong to that default segment, they will see the content that's currently in that editable area at the moment.

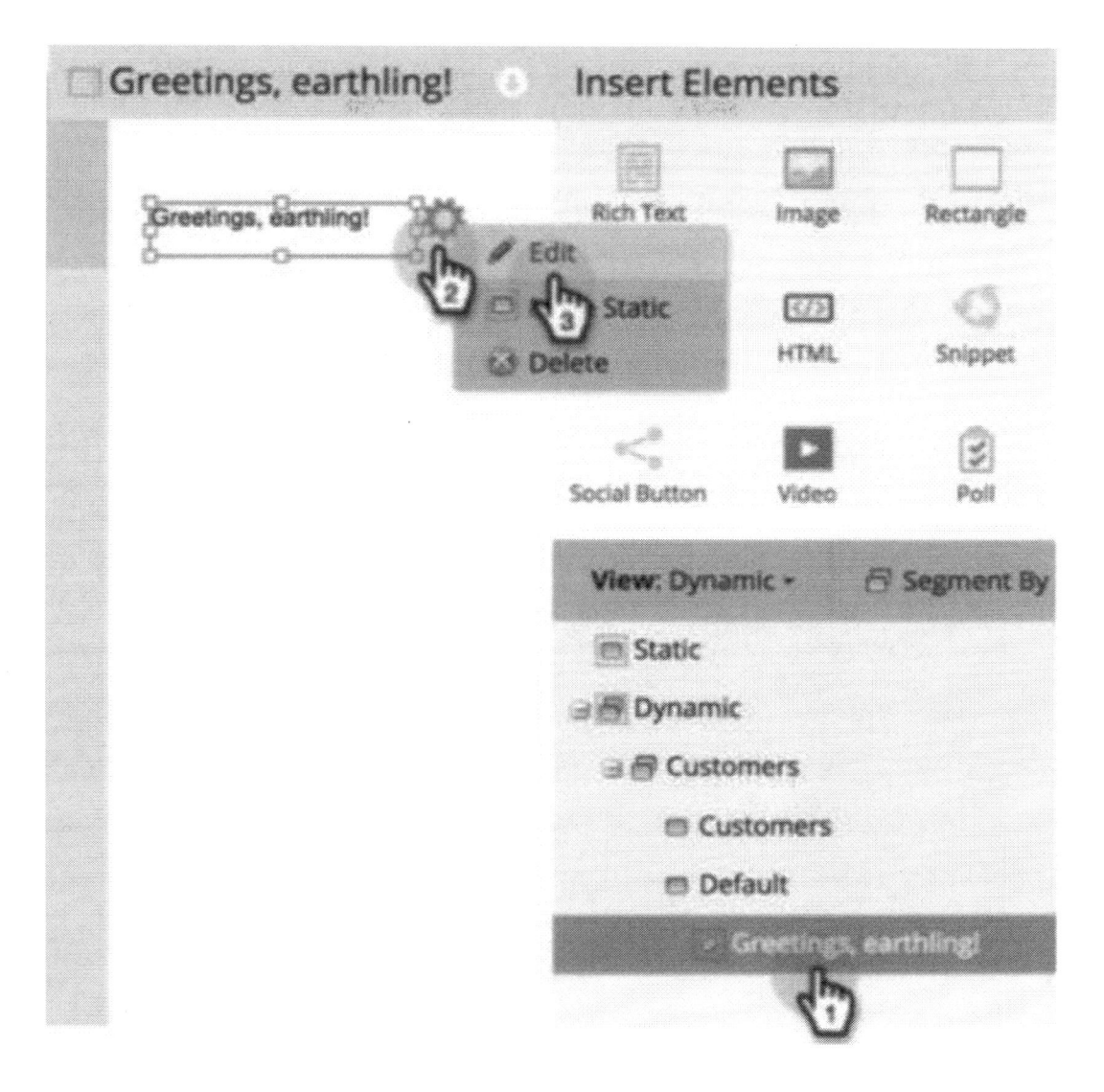

(4) On the right, select any another segment and click on the same editable area item you are making dynamic to edit it again. For example, if the other segment is "prospects", make sure to select it on the right so the editable area turns yellow briefly again. Then, click into the text and make another textual change, such as "Test Example". Then save the new text and associate it to the "prospect" segment. Try

clicking between the prospect and customer segments on the right of the landing page editor and notice how the text in the same editable are changes automatically!

(5) Now, repeat for all other editable areas and segments as needed to personalize each asset.

(6) Click Save & Approve.

Leveraging Dynamic Content when sending newsletters, nurture or drip-campaign emails, building landing pages, and other assets that you'll need will allow you to personalize them for each person or account your marketing to. Again, this is a HUGE time saver and those organizations that learn how to leverage dynamic content for their prospects find the most success when using Marketo to its fullest!

Chapter 3 – Nurture Programs & Strategy

Nurture programs are one of Marketo's flagship program types that allow you to easily create nurture/drip campaigns for different prospect segments. It's easy to get carried away with all the different bells and whistles that the nurture program-type offers, and many marketing teams initially get overwhelmed with how to set these up correctly. As you can imagine, there are countless nurture programs that you can build for a variety of reasons, based on your organization's marketing strategy. In this chapter, we'll focus on creating a set of best-practice initial nurture programs that will allow you to start nurturing your prospects at different stages of your marketing funnel. Feel free to customize as needed, but the general concepts should be similar and applied where necessary.

First, I'd like to begin with a diagram that helps outline this strategy. It's mainly designed for content-mapping to plan internally the best content pieces for each of the recommended programs that will be built. The following also provides a great internal-working-doc that teams can collaborate and be aligned on:

(Programs)	Stream 1	Stream 2	Stream 3	Default
TOFU				
MOFU				
BOFU				

Reviewing at the diagram above, the left-column represents three different nurture programs. Each nurture program should represent Top-of-Funnel (TOFU), Middle-of-Funnel (MOFU), and Bottom-of-Funnel (BOFU). TOFU content is typically NOT aggressive or trying to sell anything. But rather, it raises awareness of your organization and offers various thought-leadership content. MOFU content takes it to the next level and should be slightly more aggressive and funnel prospects into the sales process, such as content designed for marketing qualified leads (or MQLs). Lastly, BOFU content should be most aggressive and try to push prospects over the hump, ideally to a closed-won opportunity. Examples of BOFU content can be ROI calculators, competitor comparisons, and things that help get contracts signed!

Next, think about how you market content to prospects? It's important to have a basic understanding of this to personalize content for each segment of leads you are marketing to. The more personalized the content for each segment, the more their engagement with your emails based on the persona you're targeting. For example, think about segmenting content by product-interest, by vertical, by title or job-level, or any combination of these.

This is where this strategy will begin to differ from one organization to the next. Careful consideration about how to best structure your content will maximize your prospects' engagement with your emails. For this best-practice nurture program(s) example, let's use a simple use-case of segmenting content based on different verticals or industries.

In each nurture program you will have the ability to add multiple **streams**. A stream is a dedicated "container" that holds emails in a prioritized order that they will be sent out in. Its worth noting that in any nurture program you can have **up to 25 streams**. Each stream should be titled based on the industry that the emails and content within it are made for. Using the diagram above, lets assume that stream-1 is for the Healthcare industry, stream-2 is for Retail, and stream-3 is for Automotive. Once any prospect enters the nurture program, Marketo will determine what stream they should fall under and in turn what content best fits their industry. Now you're building and automating a much more personalized experience for your marketing leads!

The Default Stream is a best practice methodology that should be included in any Nurture Program that segments content for specific prospects. Its purpose is needed in the event any new prospects enter a nurture program but do not match any of the industries that each stream has been dedicated for. Think of it like a "catch-all" bucket where your nurture strategy leaves "no lead left behind". The content in the default stream should be more generalized to accommodate prospects from any industry, yet still showcase your organization's value propositions.

To begin creating a new nurture program, title it "TOFU – Nurture Program", or something similar indicating its purpose is to nurture top-of-funnel leads for your organization. Feel free to also customize the name as needed for your organization, the segments you market to, and what makes the most sense internally. Then, click on the **"Streams"** tab and begin building streams similar to the below configuration:

TOFU – NURTURE PROGRAM

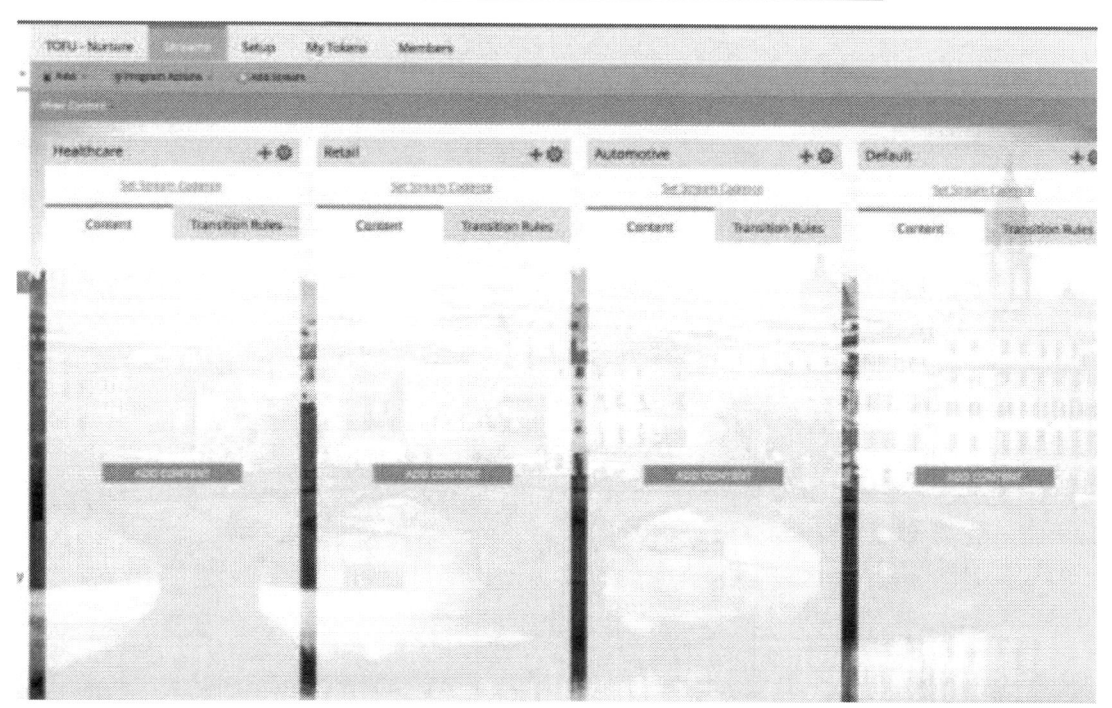

There are "**Transition Rules**" for each stream that allow prospects to transition from one stream to another if they qualify for the criteria that you set. You will need to create a transition rule for each stream (***except*** the default stream) in the event a prospect enters the program and falls into that "catch-all-bucket" and later their industry becomes known. Prospects can then easily transition into a stream that matches their industry and start receiving content personalized for what is more relevant to them. We will walk through this configuration in the next few sections.

So now that the nurture program is created and streams are built based on how content will be segmented for prospects, let's walkthrough the actual setup of the best-practice smart-campaigns that will automate everything:

(1) First, create two folders under the nurture program titled "Campaigns" and "Local Assets"

        TOFU - Nurture

           Campaigns

           Local Assets

(2) In the campaigns folder, create a new smart-campaign called "**01-Add to Nurture**". Then, in the smart-list tab, use the below logic:

Smart List Tab Criteria

(1) Trigger: Person is Created (No Constraints).
(2) Filter: Member of Smart List – in – "Marketable Persons" – (Discussed in previous chapter)
(3) Filter: "Person Status" - not contains – "MQL, SAL, SQL, Customer"

**Note- for those who aren't familiar with the above abbreviations, MQL stands for Marketing Qualified Lead, SAL stands for Sales-Accepted, and SQL is meant for Sales-Qualified. All organizations have some variation of these statuses depending on their marketing maturity level.

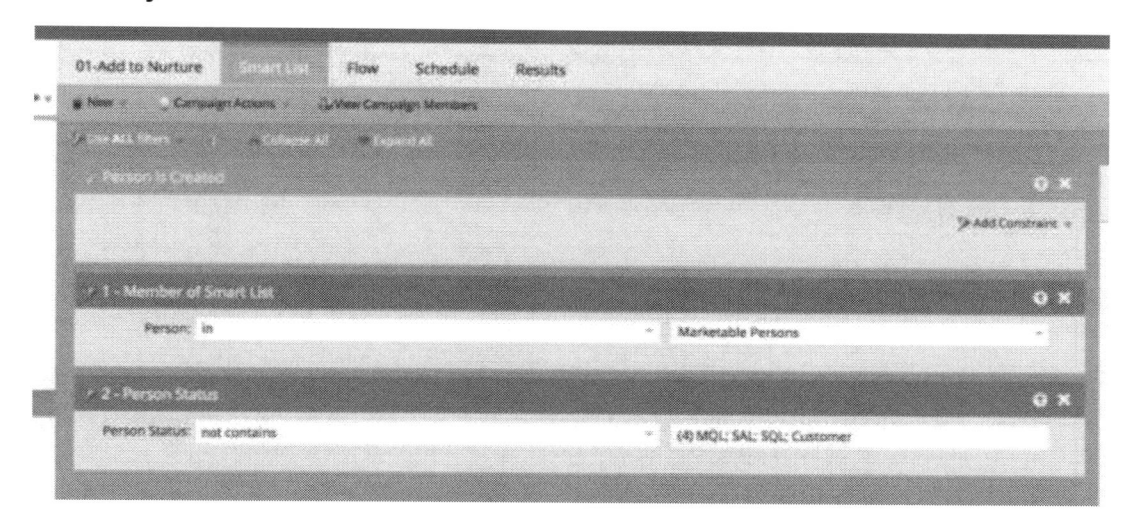

![Smart List screenshot showing filters: Person is Created, Member of Smart List (Person in Marketable Persons), and Person Status (not contains (4) MQL; SAL; SQL; Customer)]

You'll want to capture every new record that enters Marketo, so the first trigger used will simply pull in net-new leads as soon as they are created. Remember, no lead left behind! The second filter is to ensure they have a valid email, aren't blacklisted or unsubscribed upon entry or any other reason(s) defined in the "Marketable Persons" smart-list. The third filter ensures they're not created further down the funnel and added to the TOFU (top of the funnel) nurture. It will be awkward to send prospects who are ready to by top-of-funnel content so it's vital to ensure that the content sent to prospects matches where they are in their buyer's journey. The person-status field is referenced in the smart-list to serve as an example of any field your organization may use to stamp a record that's further down in the funnel. If there are separate custom fields used for this purpose, or fields that mark leads or contacts as customers (or part of accounts marked as customers) we'll want to ensure we exclude them for entering your prospect nurture programs as well. The key takeaway is to use any additional logic that may be necessary to exclude or suppress certain types of persons that aren't actually prospects (students, etc.,) from entering into the campaigns or streams.

Now, let's proceed to the **Flow Tab Criteria:**

(1) Add to Engagement Program

A. After bringing in the flow step, create as many **"add-choices"** as there are streams.

B. Using the above examples by industry, the breakdown of this flow step would have 3 add-choice options. The bottom default choice option will be used to add prospects into the default stream.

C. How the first add-choice will look is "if" the field "industry" contains "healthcare, hospitals, medical," etc., then prospects will be added to the stream titled "Healthcare".

D. For the second add-choice, "if" the field "industry" contains "Retail" etc., then prospects will be added to the stream titled "Retail".

E. For the third add-choice, "if" the field "industry" contains "Automotive, Auto, Cars," etc., then prospects will be added to the stream titled "Automotive".

F. Lastly, for the bottom default choice option select the "Default" stream. This is for prospects who don't have their industry field populated to any of the aforementioned values will be placed.

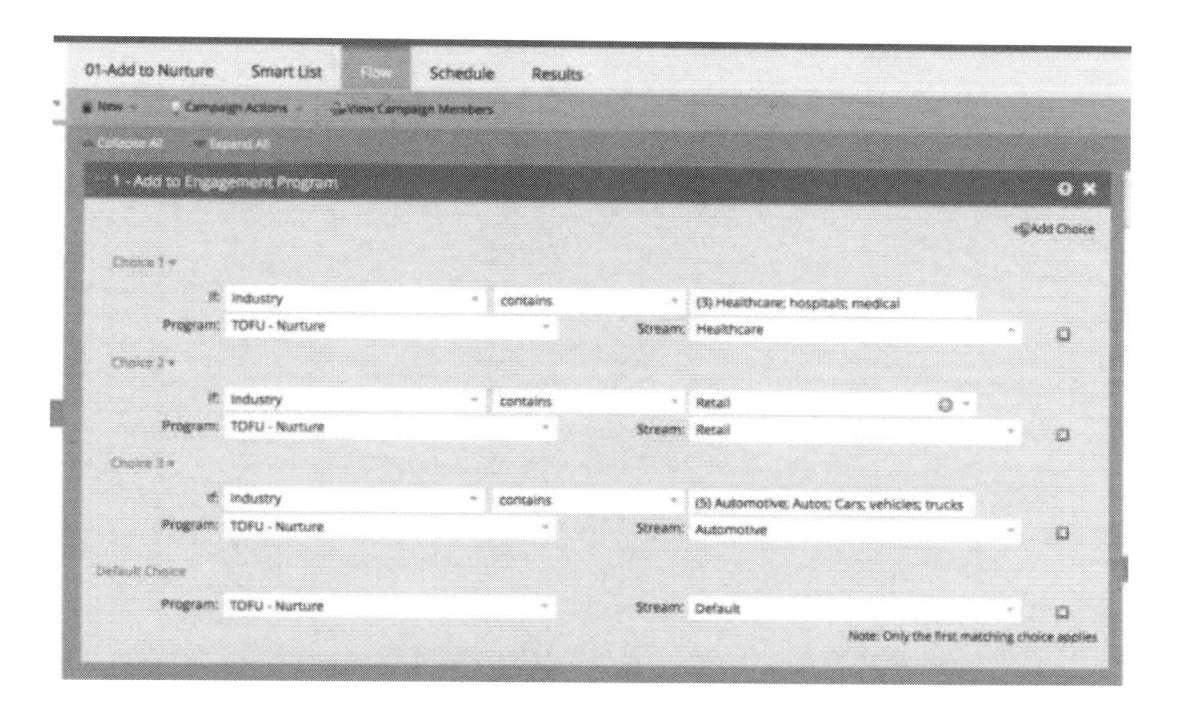

It's important to understand how the above smart-campaign functions. It's also equally important to note that if the industry field isn't being captured on any forms or as a mandatory field in CRM when creating new leads and contacts, most prospects will fall into the default stream which would not be ideal. To create the personalization that's relevant to your prospects, your data hygiene based on the segments you've chosen should be as clean as possible and continually populated for net-new people entering the database. If your marketing programs and assets lack the ability to capture critical data points needed for your organization's nurture programs, this program will not be as efficient.

Now that the first recommended smart-campaign is built, let's navigate back to the program and click on the streams tab located at the top of the page:

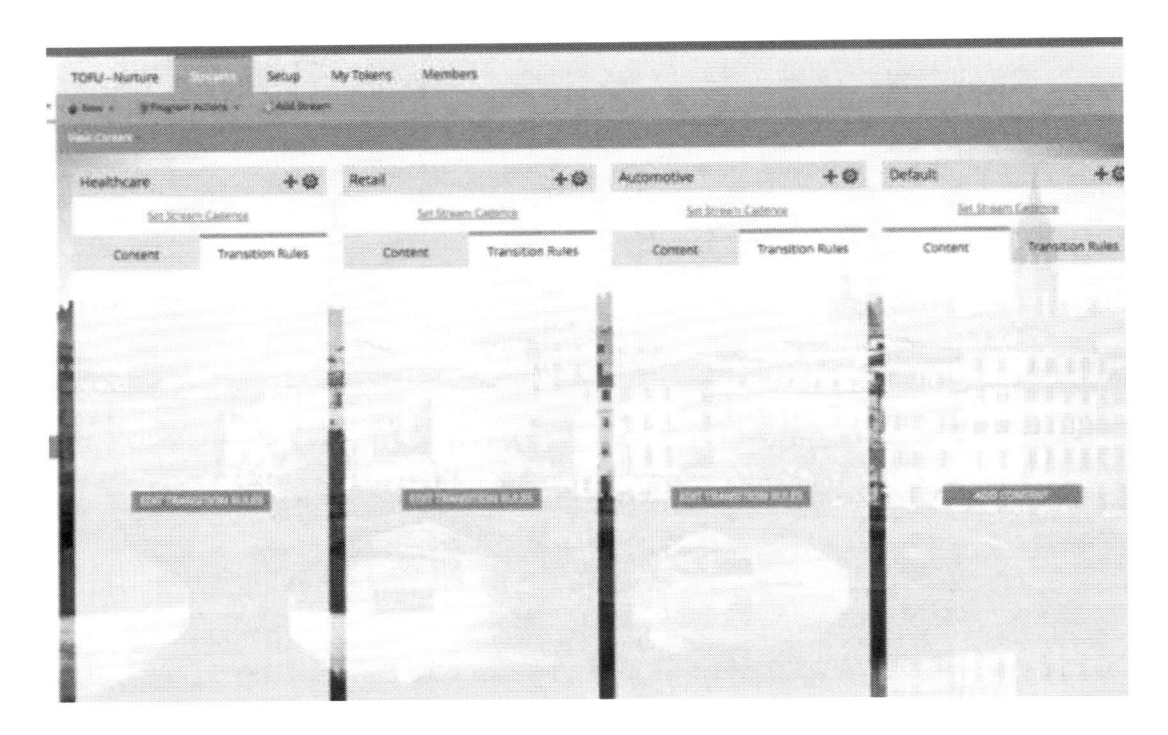

You'll want to create logic for each streams (**with the exception of the default stream**) that will enable any prospect to transition out of the default stream (**if they were added to the default stream due to their industry field being empty upon acquisition into Marketo**) once their industry field populates to match one of the values configured to drop them into a dedicated stream.

Click into the transition rule for every stream being built, except the default stream. The reason for this lies in the fact that transition rules work similar to a home vacuum-cleaner. You're building rules for each stream that determine how leads and contacts will get "sucked" into that stream. If they qualify. The reasoning for not creating a transition rule for the default stream itself is simply due to there being rare occasions where a prospect needs to transition into the default stream after already being placed into a dedicated stream. So long story short, no need to create a transition rule for that.

Once you click on the transition rule button for any stream, another tab in your browser will open. It will resemble a simple smart campaign with only the smart-list and flow tabs available. Again, I can't stress enough how many teams and Marketo customers seem to get confused here, and it's a confusing section for sure! The way to think about each transition rule is "what rule will make a person come into this stream" vs "these are the rules I'm building that will cause someone to exit this stream". This is the main misconception and mistake made when building transition rules. Think of it like a vacuum cleaner sucking people into it rather than blowing people out.

Let's build a transition rule for the healthcare stream. The smart-list will resemble the below logic and keep in mind that all transition rules **require** at least one trigger to function properly:

Transition Rule Smart-List:

Trigger: Data Value Changes - Use the field "**Industry**" & Add a constraint for "**New Value**" which contains "healthcare, health, medical," etc., or basically all the values specified that would cause someone to enter this stream upon entry into Marketo

Filter - There will be a system default filter that you cannot edit, which states that the lead or contact entering into this stream has to be a part of this nurture program and cannot be in this same stream at the moment.

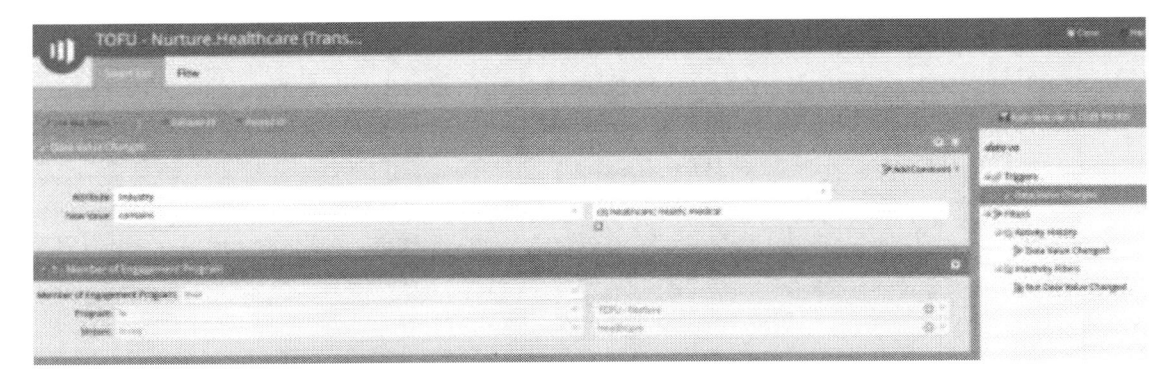

Now, the flow tab is relatively set up and ready to go. There is typically no need to add anything into here as an additional flow unless you have a specific reason. If a person meets the smart list criteria, they will be added into this stream and will begin receiving content in that stream. Simple as that!

Once you exit out of the transition rule screen and browser tab, you'll need to repeat the above process for every single stream you have, but again **with the exception of the default stream**.

After completing the transition rules for your different streams, let's move on to our second best-practice smart campaign. Navigate back to the smart campaigns folder and create a second smart campaign titled "**02-Pause Nurture**".

This specific campaign will pause prospects in streams based on any activity that is deemed required for people to stop receiving content. For example, since this entire nurture program's purpose is to nurture leads at the top of the funnel, one example of a pause-criteria is once people reach MQL (or Marketing Qualified Lead, as per your Marketing teams definition) you'll probably want to pause them in the stream they're in so they can move into the middle of the funnel (MOFU) nurture program that you'll want to create. The thinking behind this is that those prospects nearing "qualification" shouldn't be receiving top-of-funnel content which typically raises awareness of your organization.

There may be other criteria that deems leads and contacts as an MQL as well, for example lead scoring which we will discuss in the next chapter. If a person reaches your scoring threshold, they're now an MQL too. Or, you may have other "fast-tracks" to an MQL such as prospects converting off of a demo request form, or something that indicates an immediate MQL without needing to accumulate scoring that adds up to your MQL threshold. Think through this portion to ensure you've captured as many scenarios as possible. The recommended smart list should look like the below:

Smart List Tab Criteria

(1) Trigger: Score is Changed – Use the "Person Score" field which sums up both behavior scores and demographic scores. Then, **add a constraint** for a "new score" to at least **"enter your MQL threshold"** (if this has not been completed yet, read through the next chapter on lead scoring and determining your MQL threshold). For the below example, we'll use 100 as a baseline.

(2) Trigger: Data Value Changes - on the field "Person Status" to (add a constraint for "New Value" is "MQL")

(3) Filter: Member of Engagement Program: (It should auto-populate this specific nurture program's name) - to ensure only members from this nurture program get added to the flow step: - (with the **constraint** for program cadence) where the program cadence is currently "normal" (meaning only allow leads who are not paused at this moment)

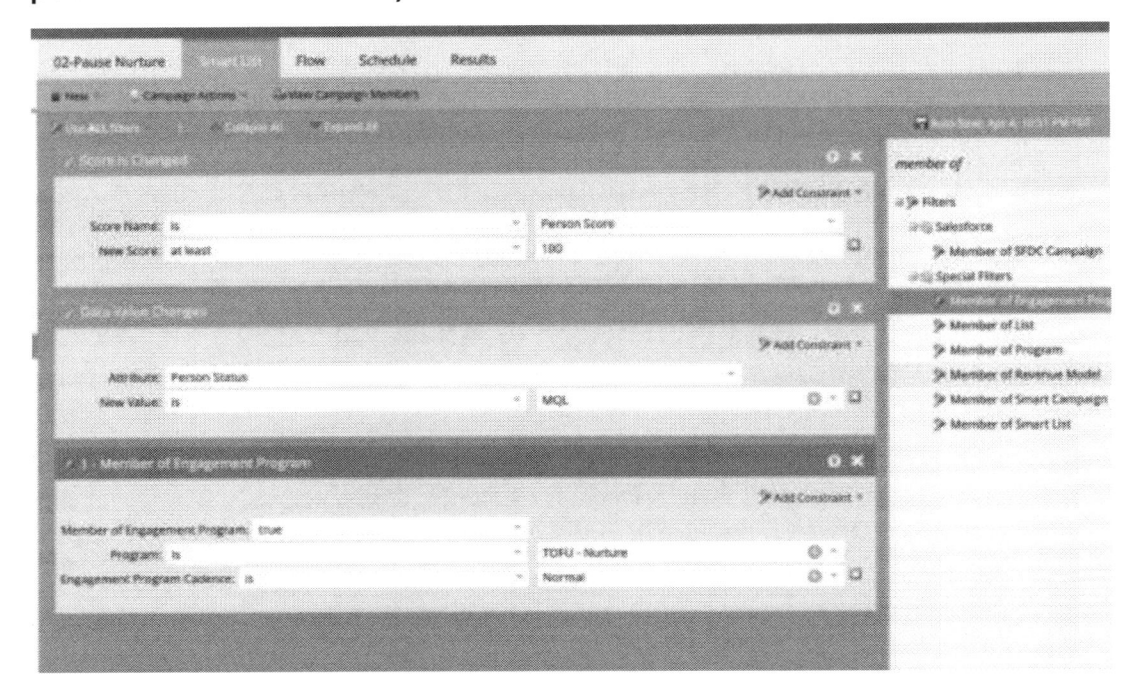

Once you have added your required logic, proceed to the flow tab:

Flow Tab Criteria:

(1) Change Engagement Program Cadence - to equal - **"Paused"**

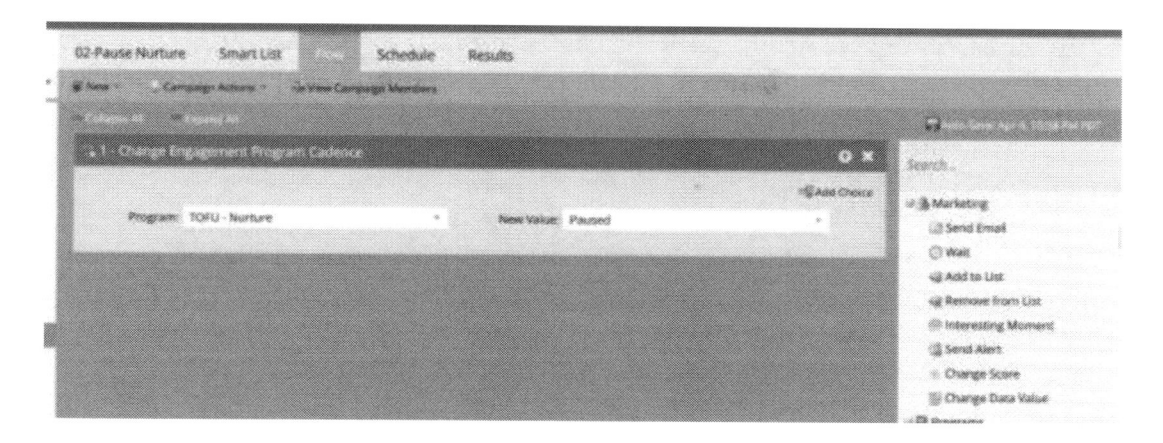

Now, this smart-campaign will indefinitely pause a person in the stream they are currently in once they meet the criteria. This will auto-prevent them from receiving any further top-of-funnel content. Now let's think about a scenario where you may want to resume a person who was once paused. For example, let's say that a person who was moved to MQL status was then moved into a "recycled" status meaning they aren't ready to be passed to a sales person yet. If a sales development rep gets on a phone with this prospect to learn they aren't ready to proceed yet in their buyer's journey, they may want to throw that prospect back into the same TOFU nurture if the content still fits to where they are in the buying process.

To create this third best-practice smart campaign, lets navigate back to the smart campaigns folder and create a third smart campaign titled "**03-Resume Nurture**".

We'll use the above "recycle" status example for the smart campaign configuration but note that there may be other custom requirements relevant to your organization that can be included. Or, you may feel this particular campaign isn't best for your nurture strategy and may want to altogether skip it. In my experience, it's good to set this up to ensure that prospects have a way to re-enter the same program and stream they originated from, just in case. Also, if they re-enter, they will simply pick up where they left off. They will not start from the top of the stream nor receive any of the emails that have already been sent to them. The smart campaign setup should look like the following:

Smart List Tab Criteria

(1) Trigger: Data Value Changes: on the "Person Status" field to equal "Recycled" with the **constraint** that the prior person status was "MQL"

(2) Trigger: Data Value Changes: on the "Contact Status" field to equal "recycled" with the **constraint** that the prior contact status was "MQL"

(3) Filter: Member of Engagement Program: (It should auto-populate this specific nurture program's name) and add a constraint for program cadence to be set to **"Paused"**. This will only consider leads who have been paused and recycled to be resumed back into the nurture program, right where they left off at.

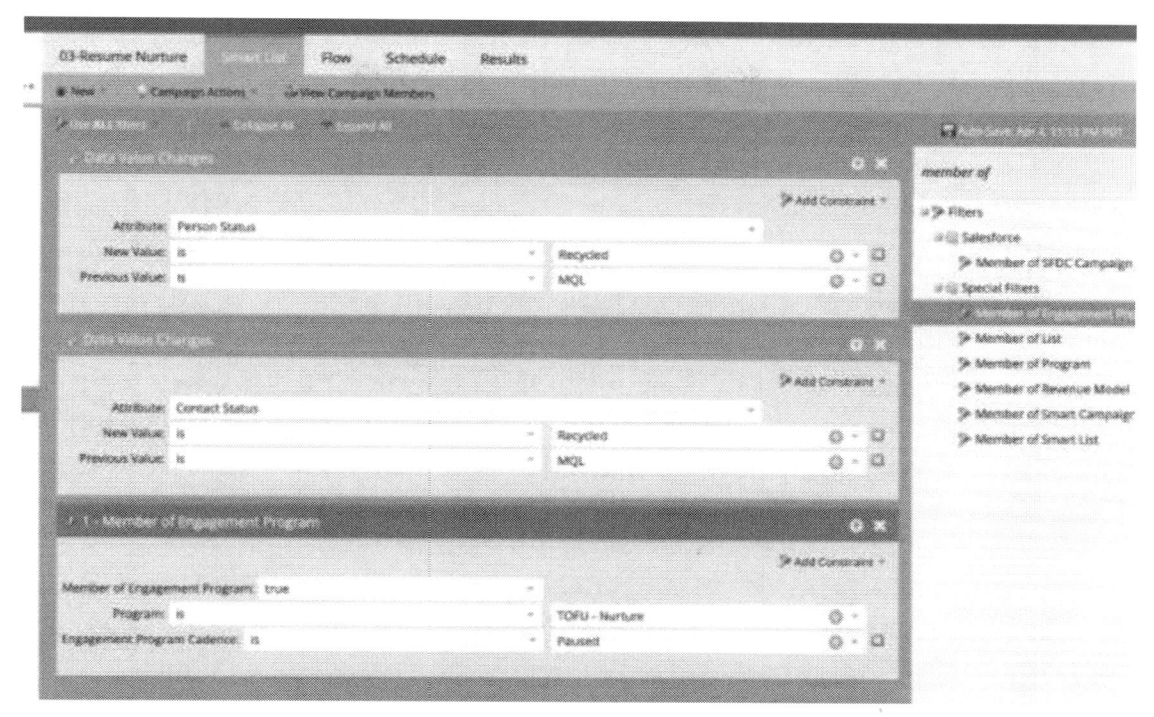

When any person qualifies for the above criteria, they will proceed to the flow tab.

Flow Tab Criteria:

(1) Change Engagement Program Cadence - to equal - "**Normal**"

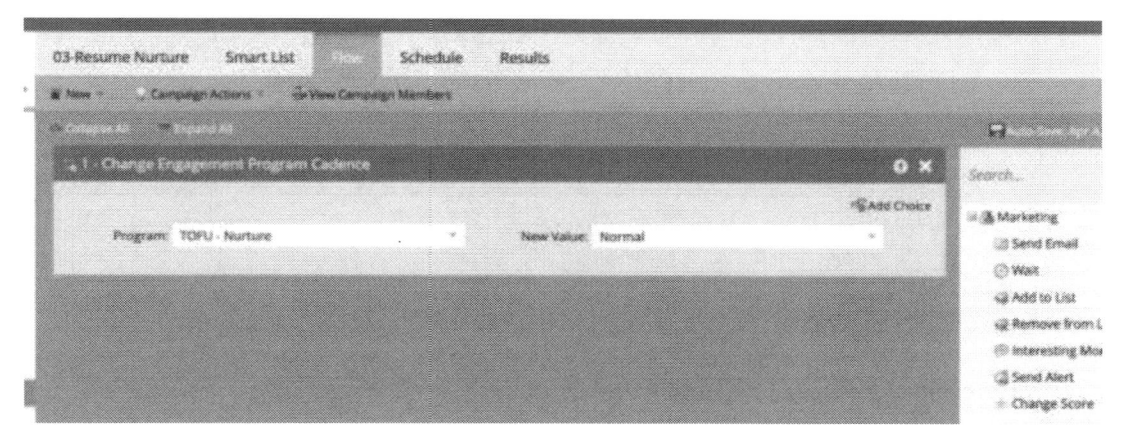

Lastly, we'll want to think about capturing the success of this nurture program. Success in Marketo means that a prospect has reached the goal of the program that you have built. To give this program credit as a success, we'll want to think about the purpose of this program overall, the same as you would to all your Marketo programs.

Again, this type of nurture program is meant to nurture people who are top of the funnel until they reach your organization's "middle of the funnel" criteria. So typically, it will duplicate the same criteria as your pause-campaign that we discussed above. Aside from reaching your pause-criteria, such as hitting MQL, reaching your threshold, etc., to give this program credit, we want to ensure that the lead or contact interacted with the program in some way or another. Since most nurture programs mainly consists of emails being sent on a regular cadence, most organizations consider engagement as clicking into an email.

You can customize what's considered success using any filter or triggers, but in most cases, you'll want to give this program credit if a person **is paused, and if and only if they clicked into any of the emails inside the stream**. Again, "success" status is mainly used for understanding program performance as well as attribution (equal-touch, first touch, etc.,). You really want to ensure that you are giving this program credit accurately to understand later down the road whether this nurture had any impact on your newer prospects and eventually on your opportunities and bottom line.

To create this fourth, and final, best-practice smart campaign, lets navigate back to the smart campaigns folder and create a fourth smart campaign titled "**04-Success**".

The smart-list criteria would resemble the below configuration:

Smart List Tab Criteria

(1) Trigger: Score is Changed – Use the "Person Score" field which sums up both behavior scores and demographic scores. Then, **add a constraint** for a "new score" to at least "**enter your MQL threshold**" (again, if this has not been completed yet read through the next chapter on lead scoring and determining your MQL threshold). For this example, we'll continue to use 100 as a baseline.

(2) Trigger: Data Value Changes - on the field "Person Status" to (add a constraint for "New Value" is "MQL")

(3) Filter: Clicked Link in Email – (list out all emails in this nurture program) – and add a **constraint** for the past 90 days (or what you are referencing either for your current top-of-funnel average lifecycle).

(4) Filter: Member of Engagement Program: (It should auto-populate this specific nurture program's name) - to ensure only members from this nurture get added to the flow step: - (add the **constraint** for program cadence) where the program cadence is currently "normal" (meaning only allow leads who are not paused at this moment

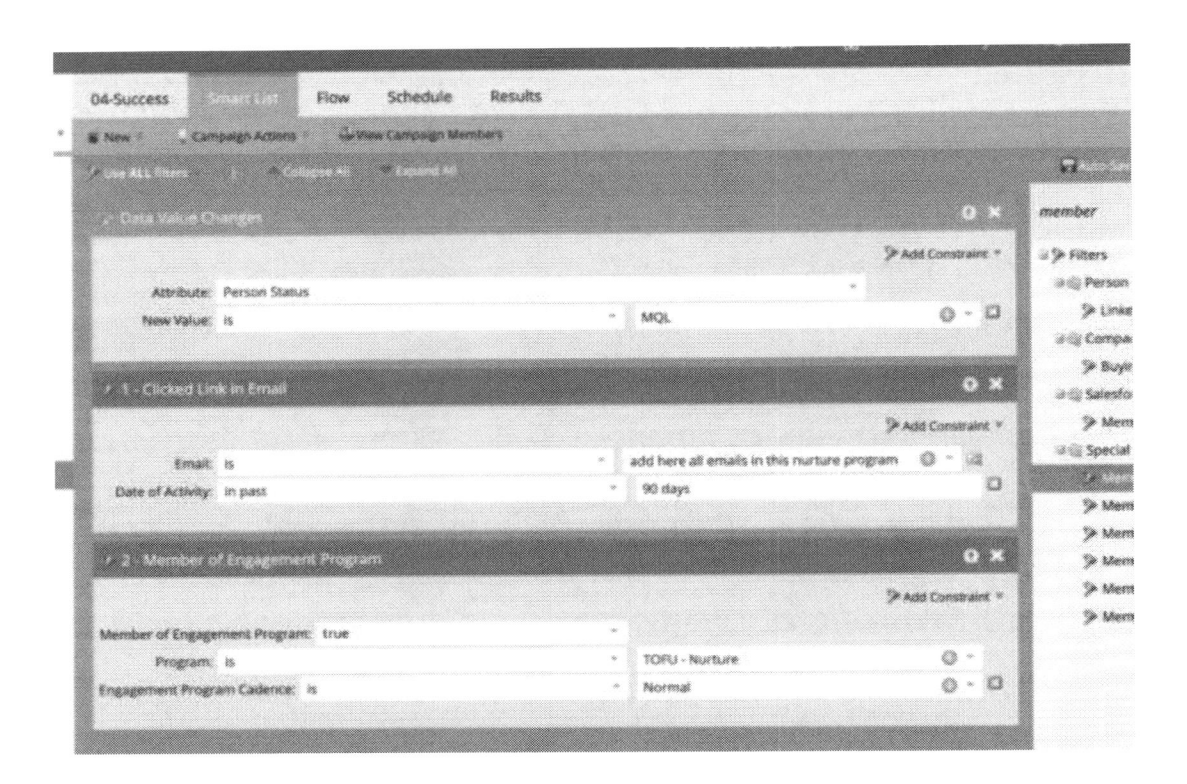

If any person qualifies for the above criteria, they will proceed to the flow tab.

Flow Tab Criteria:

(1) Change Program Status: to "Influenced" (or whatever status in the Nurture Channel represent success for your organization)

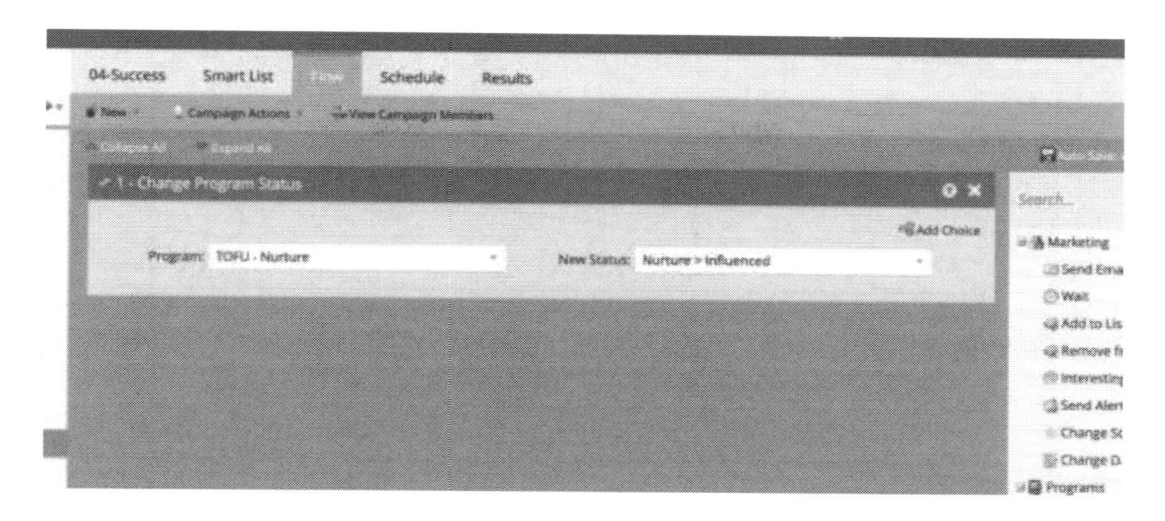

Now, the next most logical question you're probably thinking is "ok, now since my prospects graduated from the TOFU (top of the funnel) nurture, how do they get into the MOFU (Middle of the Funnel) nurture program? Glad you asked!

Since they've been "indefinitely paused" in the prior TOFU nurture program, we're going to add another flow step into the above flow tab that will add them into the MOFU nurture program we're building for this strategy. I'd like to emphasize here that the examples that are provided in this chapter are strictly basic and ones that customers who are first starting out with Marketo typically use. If you're more advanced or have other criteria in your organization that, in this specific example, qualifies a prospect to be an MQL, you'll need to consider that criteria when building out these programs.

Basically, feel free to customize as needed but note that this is the basic foundation and framework that most marketing teams start with and build upon. To complete this flow-tab section, simply add the following additional flow step into the above flow tab to add them into your "MOFU – Nurture Program"

(2) Flow Step: "Add to Engagement Program" = (**Leave this blank for now**)

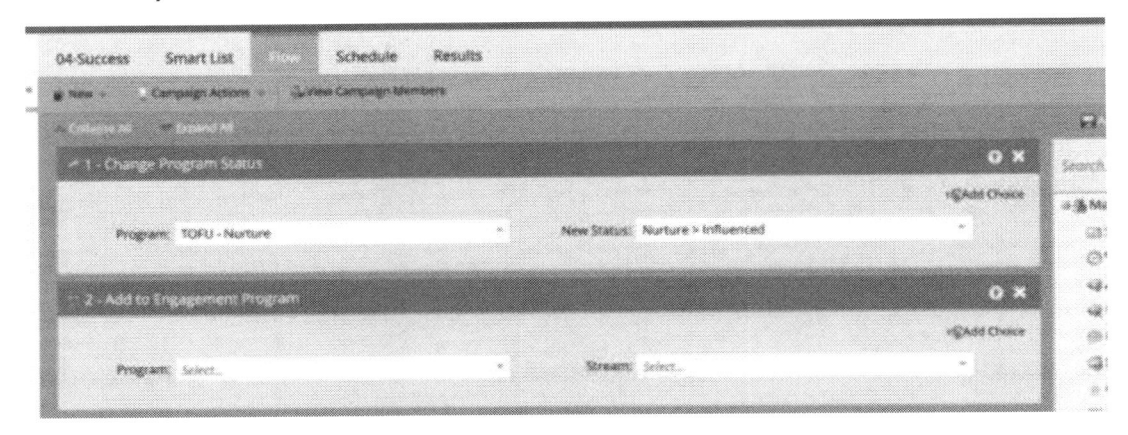

Now that you have your first "**TOFU – Nurture Program**" fully built out, don't waste any time thinking about how to build your next two programs from scratch again. Simply right-click on the TOFU nurture program and select "**Clone Program**".

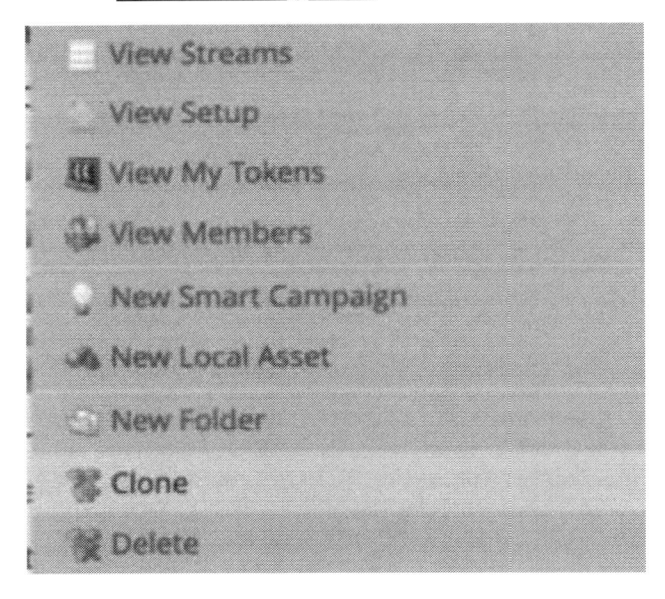

Clone the program twice.

The first time you clone it, name it "MOFU-Nurture Program". Then, clone it once more with the title of "BOFU-Nurture Program".

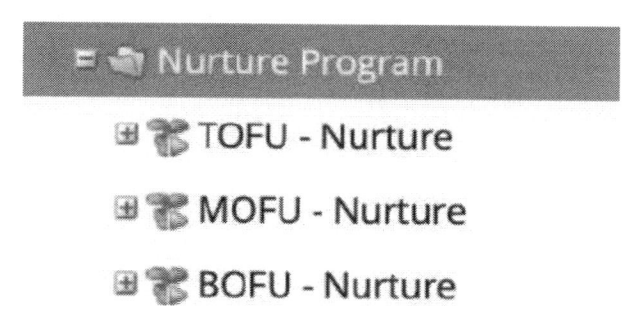

- Nurture Program
  - TOFU - Nurture
  - MOFU - Nurture
  - BOFU - Nurture

Once you've cloned the 1st nurture program, all of the campaigns and assets that were previously built will not need to be rebuilt. This saves marketing teams a ton of time not having to repeat the above steps from scratch each time and allows you to simply make minor modifications to reflect the stage of the funnel each program is made for.

The next thing you'll want to do is go back into your original "**TOFU-Nurture Program**" and navigate back into the flow step of the final "04-Success" campaign you created. In the final flow step, update the value so that once a prospect matches the criteria for "success", they will get added into the "MOFU – Nurture Program". This is how prospects get paused in one nurture indefinitely and move into the next.

You probably can see now how the rest of the two programs will be built out but let's walk through the setup together to ensure that the basic foundation is properly configured.

MOFU – NURTURE PROGRAM

Again, since the new MOFU nurture program is cloned, all of the campaigns from the prior TOFU nurture program are identical. You'll need to make some adjustments to ensure that the correct leads and contacts are being graduated into this program from the prior. For example, for the "01-Add to Nurture" smart-campaign the "Person is Created" trigger will not make sense for the middle-of-the-funnel program as people have already been in Marketo for some time.

The criteria for the "01-Add to Nurture" campaign should resemble the "02-Pause Nurture" smart-campaign criteria in the TOFU nurture program. **Because we're pausing them in the last TOFU (top of the funnel) program, the same exact criteria will be adding them into the new MOFU nurture program**.

The first smart-campaign "01-Add to Nurture" should have the following smart-list configuration:

Smart List Tab Criteria

(1) Trigger: Score is Changed – Use the "Person Score" field which sums up both behavior scores and demographic scores. Then, **add a constraint** for a "new score" to at least "**enter your MQL threshold**". For the below example, we'll use 100 as a baseline.

(2) Trigger: Data Value Changes - on the field "Person Status" to (add a constraint for "New Value" is "MQL")

(3) Filter: Member of Smart List – in – "Marketable Persons" – (Discussed in previous chapter)

(4) Filter: "Person Status" - not contains – "MCL, MEL, SAL, SQL, Customer" - The first two (MCL & MEL) represent person statuses "Marketing Captured Lead", "Marketing Engaged Lead", or those statuses for leads entering top-of-funnel" – This filter is in place to prevent accidentally adding someone to from Top of bottom of the funnels, based on their person statuses.

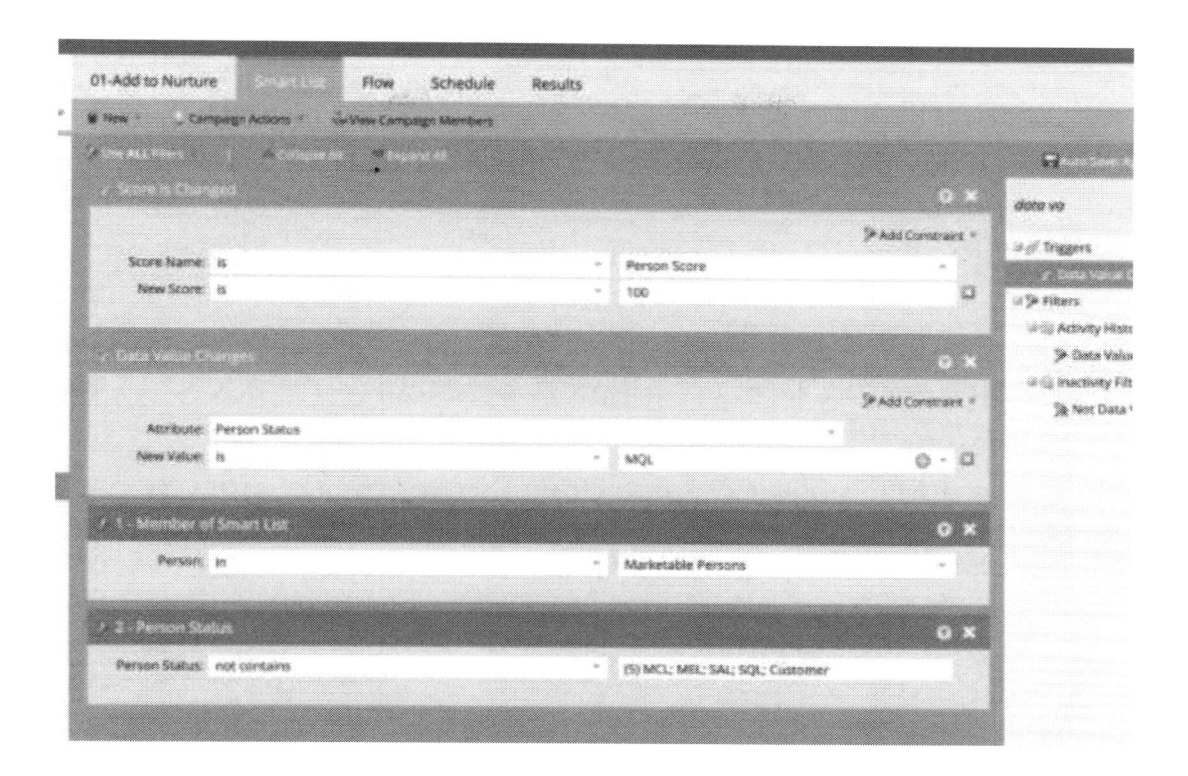

Once you have added your required logic, proceed to the flow tab. Since this is a cloned program, the flow should not have changed from the prior TOFU nurture program and should resemble the below.

Flow Tab Criteria:

(1) **Add to Engagement Program**

A. Since this is a duplicate flow step, confirm there are as many "**add-choices**" as there are streams.

B. Using the original examples "by industry", the breakdown of this flow step would have 3 add-choice options. The bottom default choice option will be used to add prospects into the default stream.

C. How the first add-choice will look is "if" the field "industry" contains "healthcare, hospitals, medical," etc., then prospects will be added to the stream titled "Healthcare".

D. For the second add-choice, "if" the field "industry" contains "Retail" etc., then prospects will be added to the stream titled "Retail".

E. For the third add-choice, "if" the field "industry" contains "Automotive, Auto, Cars," etc., then prospects will be added to the stream titled "Automotive".

F. Lastly, for the bottom default choice option select the "Default" stream. This is for prospects who don't have their industry field populated to any of the aforementioned values will be placed.

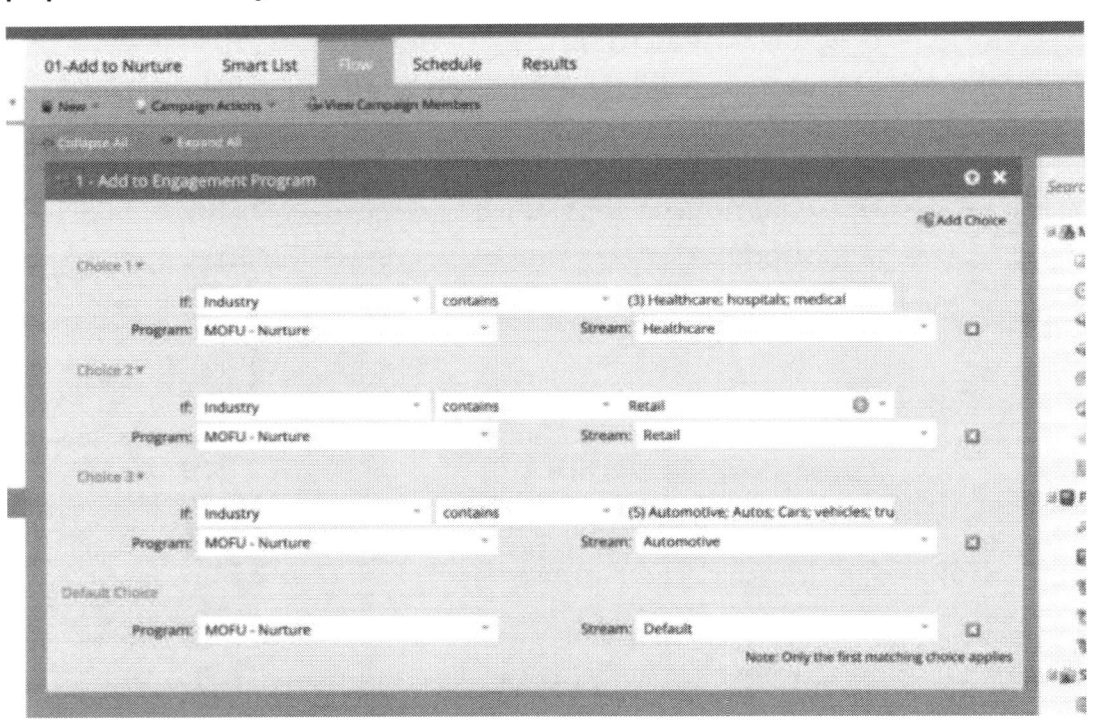

By having the cloned flow in place, the same leads and contacts who have been receiving content based on their industry in the TOFU nurture program will continue to fall into the same streams in the MOFU nurture. The difference is now they graduate to receive more targeted content designed for where they are in their buyer's journey.

The content in this nurture program should be geared towards MQLs where the intent is to get them through the middle part of your funnel. The content should be a little more "salesy" and should help nudge prospects to speak with sales about possible opportunities based on the value propositions your organization offers.

The best practice configuration for the next campaign, or the "**02-Pause Nurture**" smart-campaign should be built around what it would take an MQL to get paused in the MOFU nurture program. A common example is prospects who become part of a sales opportunity. If a prospect is added to an opportunity in your CRM, it's obvious they were accepted and qualified by sales to the point where they see a potential sales opportunity in pipeline.

That prospect is now moving lower and lower in your sales funnel and should receive content that's geared toward that specific type of lead. Being in CRM and part of an opportunity but receiving content that's meant for prospects in the top or mid funnels can be awkward for prospects. The content in the MOFU nurture program show give prospects a stronger nudge to help graduate them into the BOFU (or bottom of the funnel) nurture program. The configuration for the "**02-Pause Nurture**" campaign for the MOFU nurture program should resemble the following:

Smart List Tab Criteria:

(1) Trigger: Added to "**ANY**" Opportunity - (use a **constraint** for the opportunity stage) to equal is not "Closed-won" OR "Closed Lost" – (This indicates a prospect is added to a sales opportunity in CRM but on that still needs nurturing to close-win or until they are deemed a customer, ideally)

(2) Trigger: Data Value Changes - on the field "Person Status" to "SQL" (or Sales-Qualified-Lead)

(3) Trigger: Data Value Changes - on the field "Contact Status" to "SQL" (or Sales-Qualified-Lead)

(4) Filter: Member of Engagement Program: (It should auto-populate this specific nurture program's name) - to ensure only members from this nurture program get added to the flow step: - (with the **constraint** for program cadence) where the program cadence is currently "**normal**" (meaning only allow leads who are not paused at this moment)

** Or any additional logic and criteria to denote that a prospect that was once an MQL by your organization's definition has now progressed into a lower stage in your lead lifecycle**

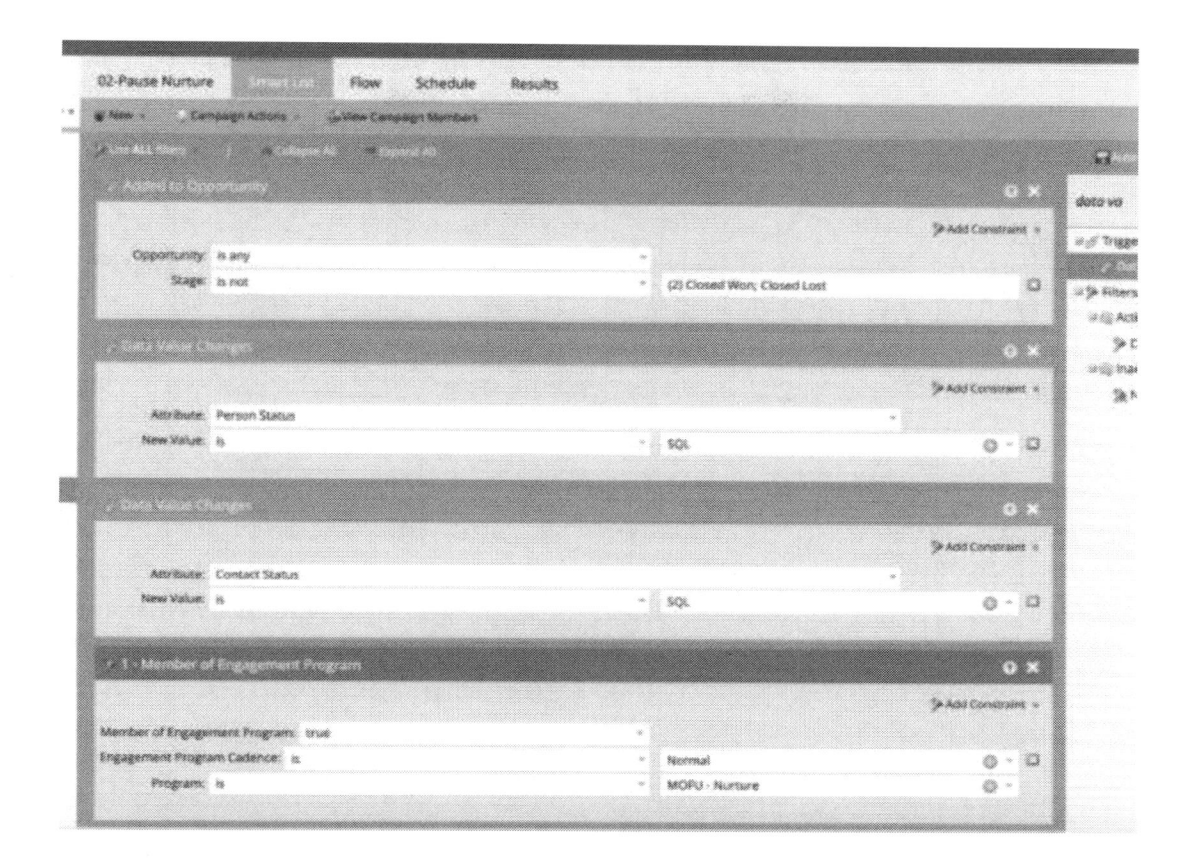

Once your required logic has been added, proceed to the flow tab:

Flow Tab Criteria:

(1) Change Engagement Program Cadence - to equal - "**Paused**"

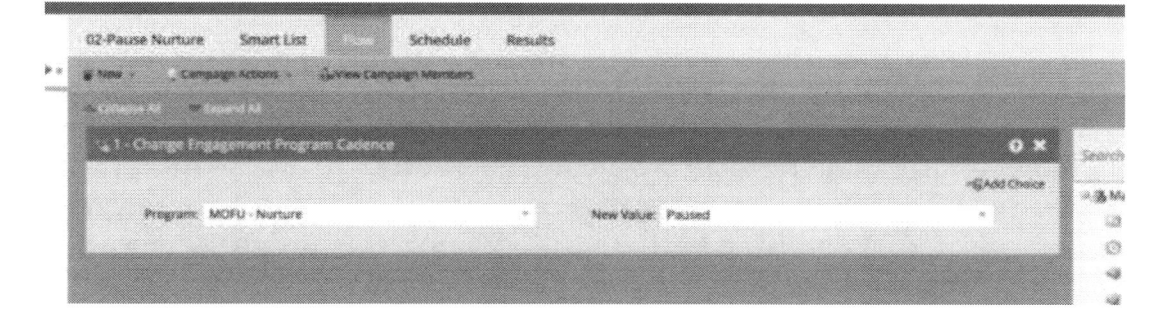

In this specific example, when a prospect is added to any opportunity, they will proceed into the next nurture program designated for the bottom of the funnel leads. But, if their status is changed to SQL (Sales Qualified Lead) and **if for whatever reason is changed back to "Recycled"**, you may consider a **"03-Resume Nurture"** smart-campaign to re-add them back! This will automate a workflow that will allow prospects to be recycled into the same nurture program that they were just paused in to continue getting nurtured until they are considered "sales-ready" again.

Majority of marketing-ops teams I've worked with feel it's best to create this additional way for prospects who are SQL but deemed "not ready" for sales to return back into the MOFU nurture to continue getting drip-emails. If this example, or other use-cases relevant to your specific organization, are applicable, then it's recommended to keep the cloned **"03-Resume Nurture"** smart-campaign and simply swap the values to resemble the below configuration:

Smart List Tab Criteria:

(1) Trigger: Data Value Changes: on the "Person Status" field to equal "Recycled" with the constraint that the previous value was "SQL" – (Meaning they were recycled

(2) Trigger: Data Value Changes: on the "Contact Status" field to equal "Recycled" with the constraint that the previous vale was "SQL"

(3) Filter: Member of Engagement Program: (It should auto-populate this specific nurture program's name) - to ensure only members from this nurture program get added to the flow step: - (with the **constraint** for program cadence) where the program cadence is currently **"Paused"** (meaning only allow leads who are paused at this moment)

[Screenshot of Smart List tab with Data Value Changes and Member of Engagement Program filters]

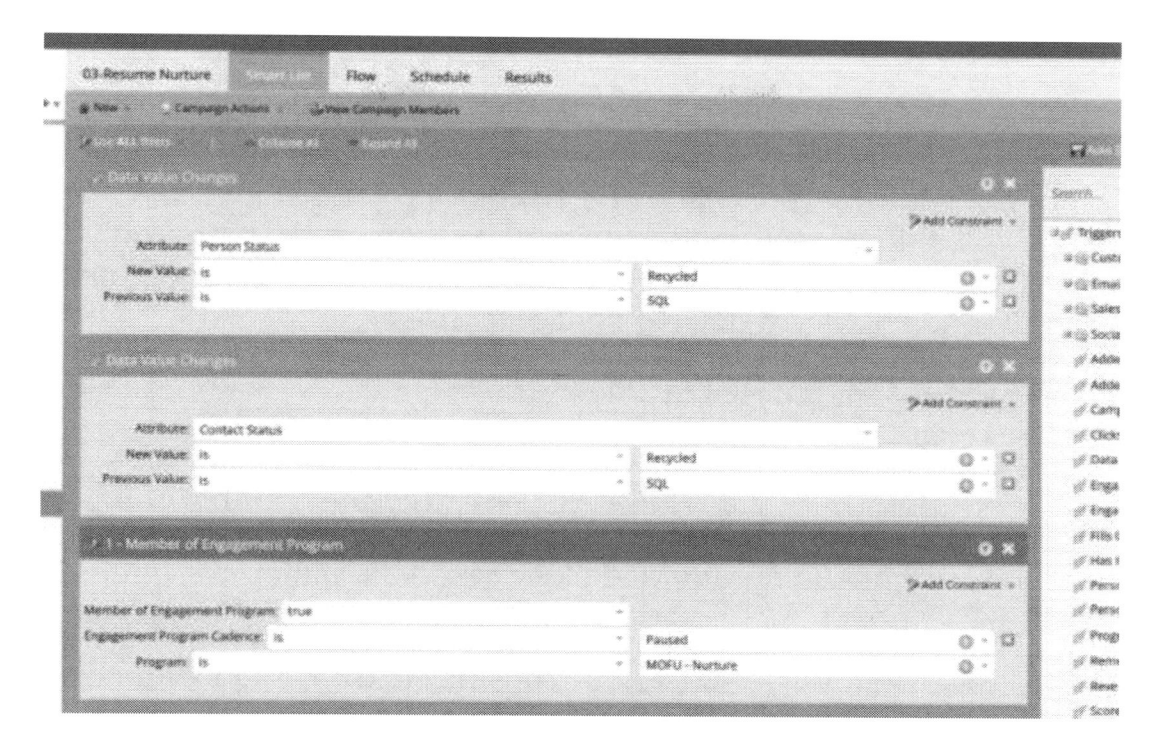

When any person qualifies for the above criteria, they will proceed to the flow tab.

Flow Tab Criteria:

(1) Change Engagement Program Cadence - to equal - "**Normal**"

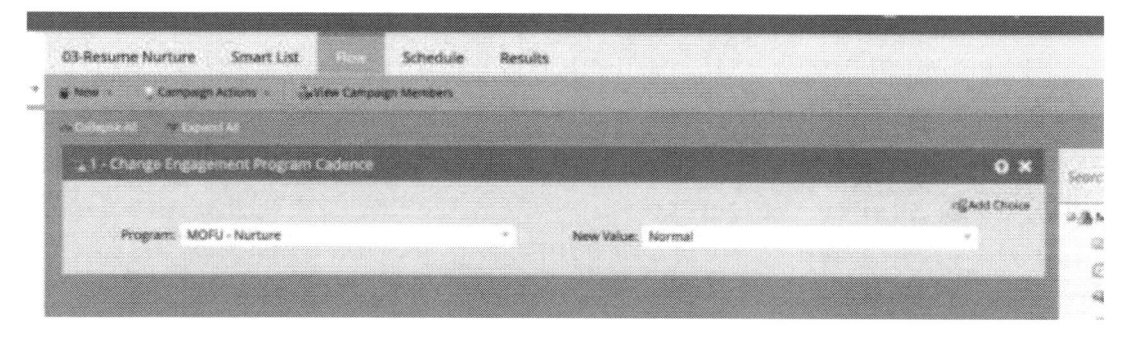

[Screenshot of Flow tab with Change Engagement Program Cadence step: Program MOFU - Nurture, New Value: Normal]

The above smart-campaign criteria will resume leads and contacts back into the MOFU program and they'll pick up right where they left off.

The last smart-campaign in the MOFU program is the success-campaign. This will follow the same exact concept from the TOFU smart-campaign by replicating the **"Pause"** criteria but ensure that we are giving success credit to this nurture program if, and only if, anyone interacts with one of the emails within. The smart campaign logic will resemble the following configuration:

Smart List Tab Criteria:

(1) Trigger: Added to "**ANY**" Opportunity - (use a **constraint** for the opportunity stage) to equal is not "Closed-won" OR "Closed Lost" – (This indicates a prospect is added to a sales opportunity in CRM but on that still needs nurturing to close-win or until they are deemed a customer, ideally)

(2) Trigger: Data Value Changes - on the field "Person Status" to "SQL" (or Sales-Qualified-Lead)

(3) Trigger: Data Value Changes - on the field "Contact Status" to "SQL" (or Sales-Qualified-Lead)

(4) Filter: Member of Engagement Program: (It should auto-populate this specific nurture program's name) - to ensure only members from this nurture program get added to the flow step: - (with the **constraint** for program cadence) where the program cadence is currently "**normal**" (meaning only allow leads who are not paused at this moment)

(5) Filter: Clicked Link in Email: - (insert all email assets that belong to this program into this filter) with the **constraint** of "Date and Time" of the last 90 days – (or whatever time frame that makes sense based on your sales cycle.)

Once you have added any additional required logic, proceed to the flow tab:

Flow Tab Criteria:

(1) Change Program Status: to "Influenced" (or whatever status in the Nurture Channel represent success for your organization)

(2) "Add to Engagement Program" = (**Leave this blank for now**)

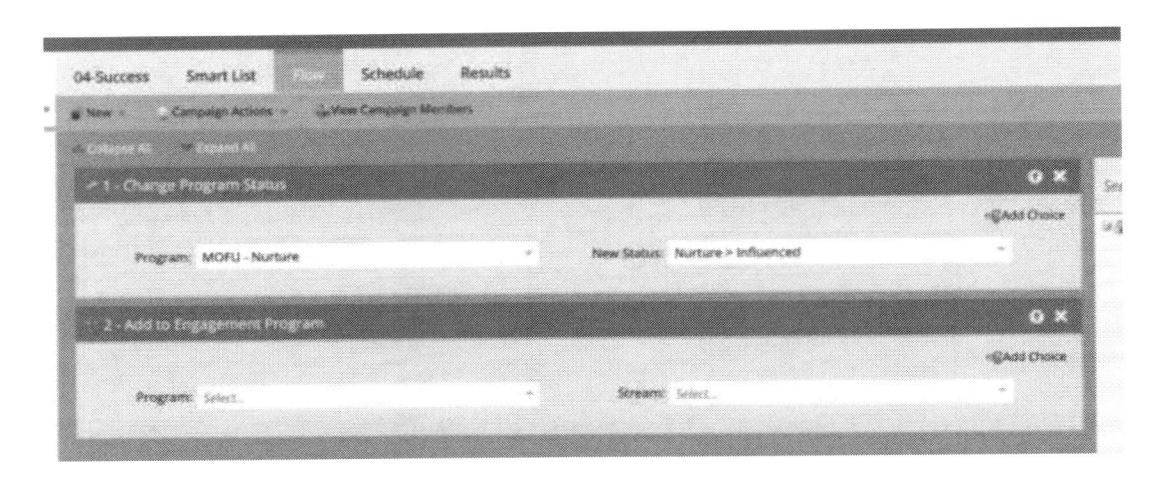

Similar to how people graduated into MOFU nurture from TOFU nurture, we'll want to consider how to architect the next nurture program for bottom of the funnel (BOFU) leads and contacts.

If you have not already, go ahead and clone the MOFU nurture program (as previously done with the TOFU nurture program) to replicate the logic in all the campaigns and save you and your team tons of time not having to rebuild from scratch.

Next, you'll want to go back into your "**MOFU-Nurture Program**" and navigate back into the flow step of the final "04-Success" campaign you created. In the final flow step, update the value so that once a prospect matches the criteria for "success", they will get added into the final "BOFU – Nurture Program". This is how middle of the funnel (MQL) prospects get paused in the MOFU nurture program indefinitely and move into the next.

BOFU – NURTURE PROGRAM

Lastly, we are building or final recommended best-practice engagement program to nurture leads and contacts who made it into an opportunity, or your organization's definition of what activities would constitute bottom of the funnel leads and contacts. The same concepts apply for this cloned nurture program in that the same prospects that is graduating from the MOFU nurture program will fall into a similar stream and receive content that's based on the industry they belong to.

The difference in content for this program compared to the MOFU nurture is that it's much more aggressive in nudging prospects to either progress through your various opportunity-stages or ideally into customers. Examples include marketing assets such as ROI calculators, competitor comparisons, and similar content that helps a hot sales opportunity convert to a new customer.

The smart campaign "01-Add to Nurture" for the BOFU nurture program will resemble the following configuration based on the prior MOFU nurture program's "pause" campaign criteria. As a reminder, the purpose for this is to pause in upper-funnel nurtures and graduate directly into lower-funnel nurtures.

Smart List Tab Criteria:

(1) Trigger: Added to "**ANY**" Opportunity - (use a **constraint** for the opportunity stage) to equal is not "Closed-won" OR "Closed Lost" – (This indicates a prospect is added to a sales opportunity in CRM but on that still needs nurturing to close-win or until they are deemed a customer, ideally)

(2) Trigger: Data Value Changes - on the field "Person Status" to "SQL" (or Sales-Qualified-Lead)

(3) Trigger: Data Value Changes - on the field "Contact Status" to "SQL" (or Sales-Qualified-Lead)

(4) Filter: Member of Smart List – in – "Marketable Persons" – (Discussed in previous chapter)

(5) Filter: "Person Status" - not contains – "MCL, MEL, MQL, SAL, Customer" - This filter is in place to prevent accidentally adding someone who is not in any of your bottom-of-the-funnel stages.

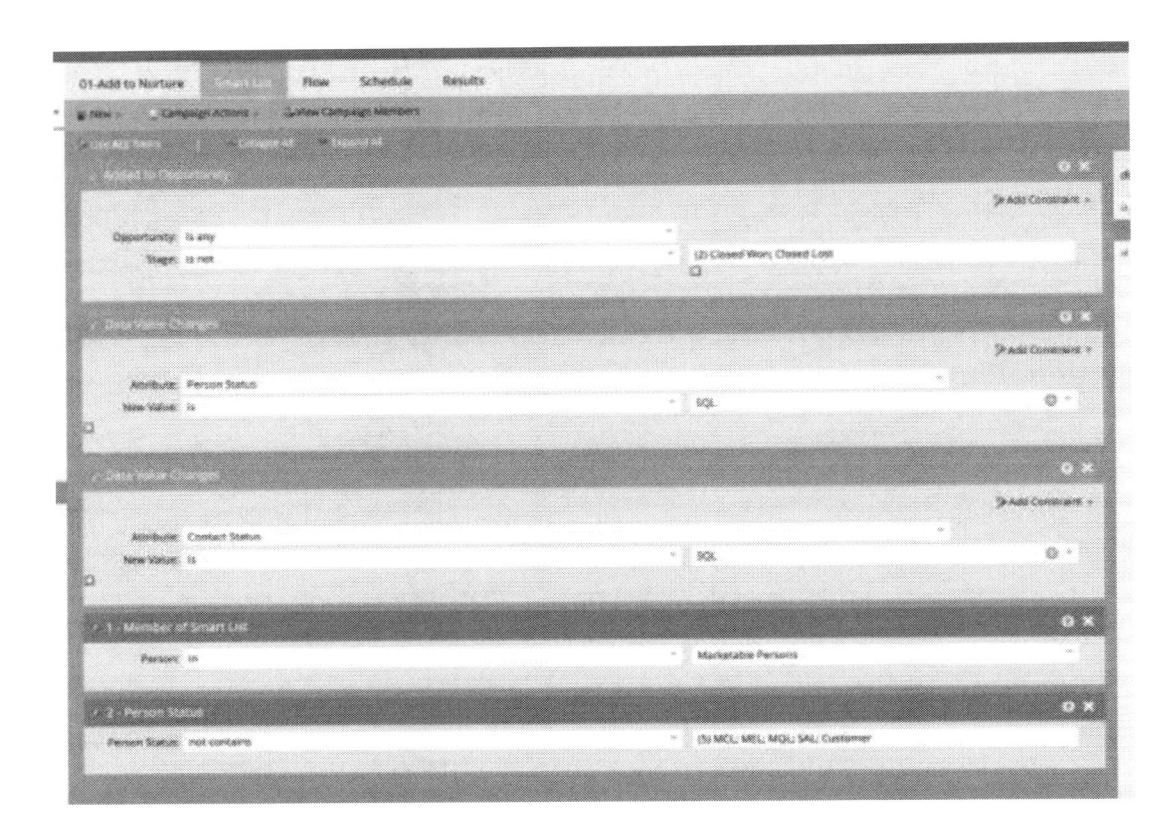

Once you have added the above required logic, proceed to the flow tab. Since this is a cloned program, the flow tab should not have changed and should resemble the below.

Flow Tab Criteria:

(1) **Add to Engagement Program**

A. Since this is a duplicate flow step, confirm there are as many **"add-choices"** as there are streams.

B. Using the original examples "by industry", the breakdown of this flow step would have 3 add-choice options. The bottom default choice option will be used to add prospects into the default stream.

C. How the first add-choice will look is "if" the field "industry" contains "healthcare, hospitals, medical," etc., then prospects will be added to the stream titled "Healthcare".

D. For the second add-choice, "if" the field "industry" contains "Retail" etc., then prospects will be added to the stream titled "Retail".

E. For the third add-choice, "if" the field "industry" contains "Automotive, Auto, Cars," etc., then prospects will be added to the stream titled "Automotive".

F. Lastly, for the bottom default choice option select the "Default" stream. This is for prospects who don't have their industry field populated to any of the aforementioned values will be

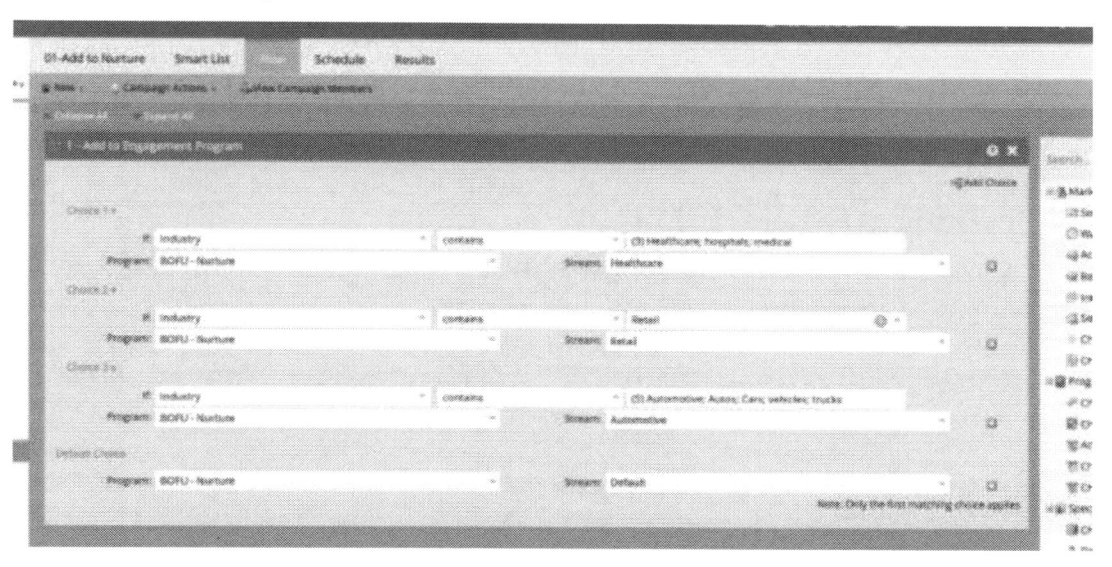

The next smart-campaign that has been cloned is again the "**02-Pause Nurture**" smart-campaign. When thinking about your BOFU nurture strategy, the purpose is to get a bottom-of-the-funnel prospect to become new-business, or a customer. **The best practice here is to have a way in CRM to denote when a customer occurs.** Since Marketo isn't reading off the account object in CRMs, it's important to have a lifecycle stage, status, or even a basic Boolean (checkbox) field that denotes whether a lead or a contact is part of an account that's considered a customer. This type of configuration, which can be modified of course, should resemble the following. To denote customers for this example, we'll use the "**Is Customer**" field. Again, your instance or data-sources may have a different custom field which will be needed.

If you're thinking about using your CRM's opportunity stages to indicate a customer, you'll want to reconsider for prospect nurtures. Since accounts can have multiple opportunities, you'll want a separate field to demote 1st time customers versus repeat customers. It's recommended you create a separate Nurture program structure to nurture customers based on the value propositions your organization offers.

Below is the recommended logic for the BOFU "02-Pause Nurture" smart-campaign:

Smart List Tab Criteria:

(1) Trigger: Data Value Changes on the "Is Customer" field to equal "TRUE"

(2) Trigger: Data Value Changes on the "Person Status" field to equal "Customer"

(3) Trigger: Data Value Changes on the "Contact Status" field to equal "Customer"

(4) Filter: Member of Engagement Program: (It should auto-populate this specific nurture program's name) - to ensure only members from this nurture program get added to the flow step: - (with the **constraint** for program cadence) where the program cadence is currently "**normal**" (meaning only allow leads who are not paused at this moment)

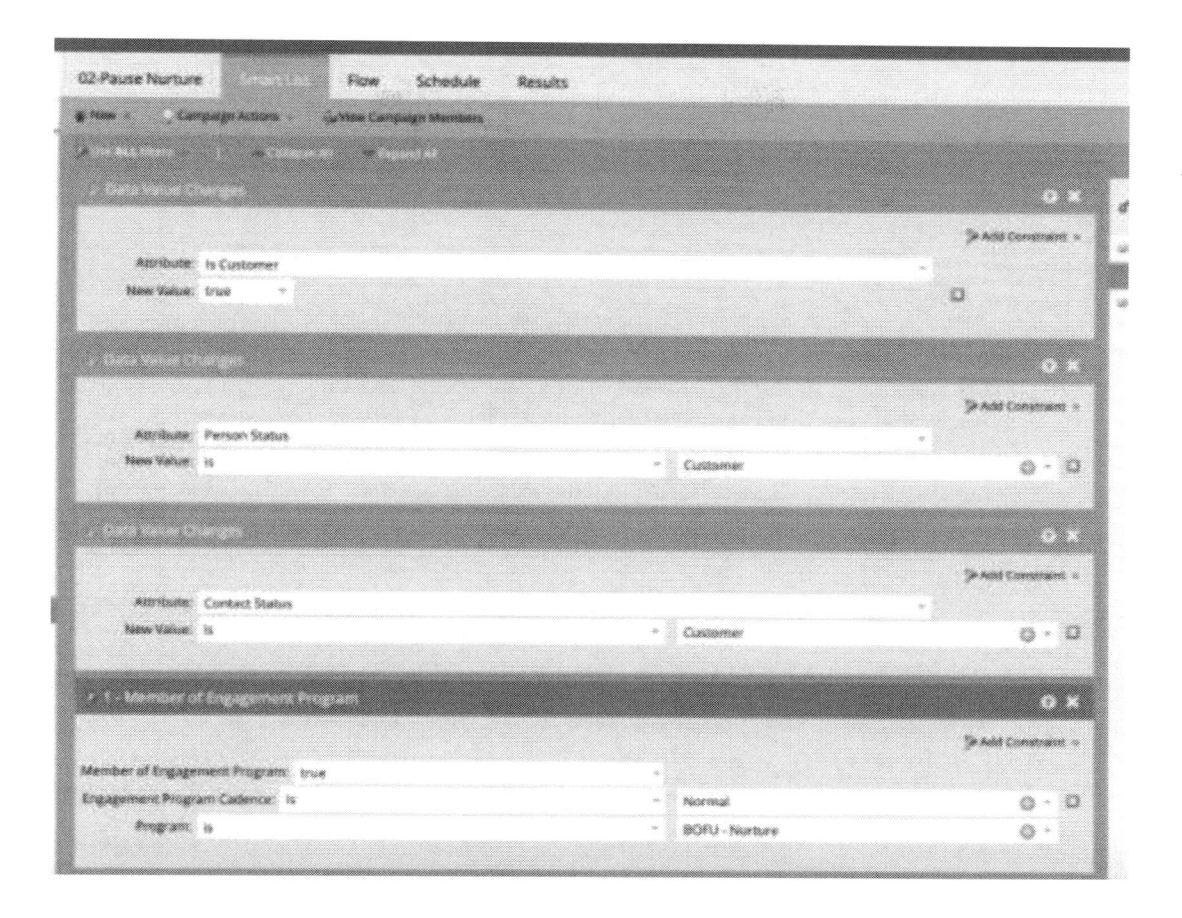

Once your required logic has been added, proceed to the flow tab:

Flow Tab Criteria:

(1) Change Engagement Program Cadence - to equal - "**Paused**"

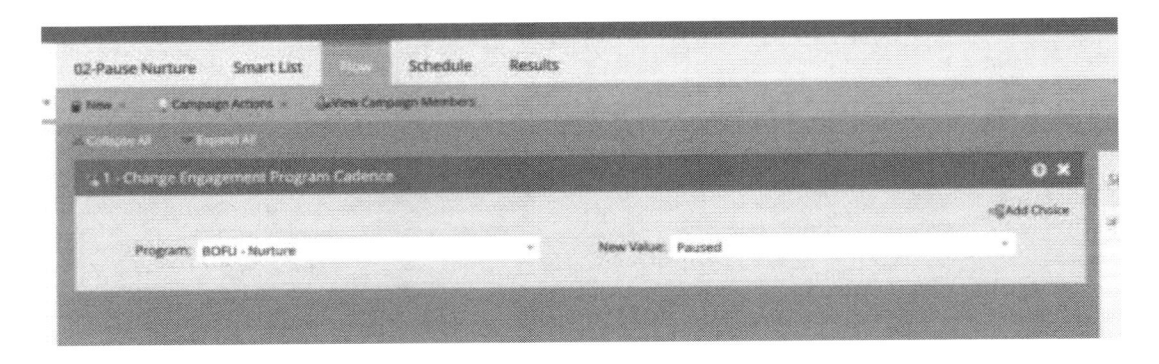

Once a prospect is part of an account that has been made into a customer in CRM, there aren't many cases where they ought to be resumed in the same *prospect* nurture program. We'll skip that in this walk-through but if your organization has such use-cases, feel free to customize as needed appropriately. Most often, it's recommended they "graduate" into a customer nurture program(s).

The next and final stage in this funnel-nurture strategy is to stamp **success** and give credit to this program if a prospect actually had some interaction with any of the content. The same configuration and concepts apply here as the previous nurture programs. We will want to consider the pause criteria in this BOFU nurture program and simply add the filter to ensure that it's given credit if, and only if, someone interacts with any of the content. The campaign's configuration should resemble the following:

Smart List Tab Criteria:

(1) Trigger: Data Value Changes on the "Is Customer" field to equal "TRUE"

(2) Trigger: Data Value Changes on the "Person Status" field to equal "Customer"

(3) Trigger: Data Value Changes on the "Contact Status" field to equal "Customer"

(4) Filter: Member of Engagement Program: (It should auto-populate this specific nurture program's name) - to ensure only members from this nurture program get added to the flow step: - (with the **constraint** for program cadence) where the program cadence is currently "**normal**" (meaning only allow leads who are not paused at this moment)

(5) Filter: Clicked link in Email – "List out all of the emails in this nurture program" – with the constraint added for "Date/Time" = in the past 90 days (or what makes most sense based on your organizations sales cycle.

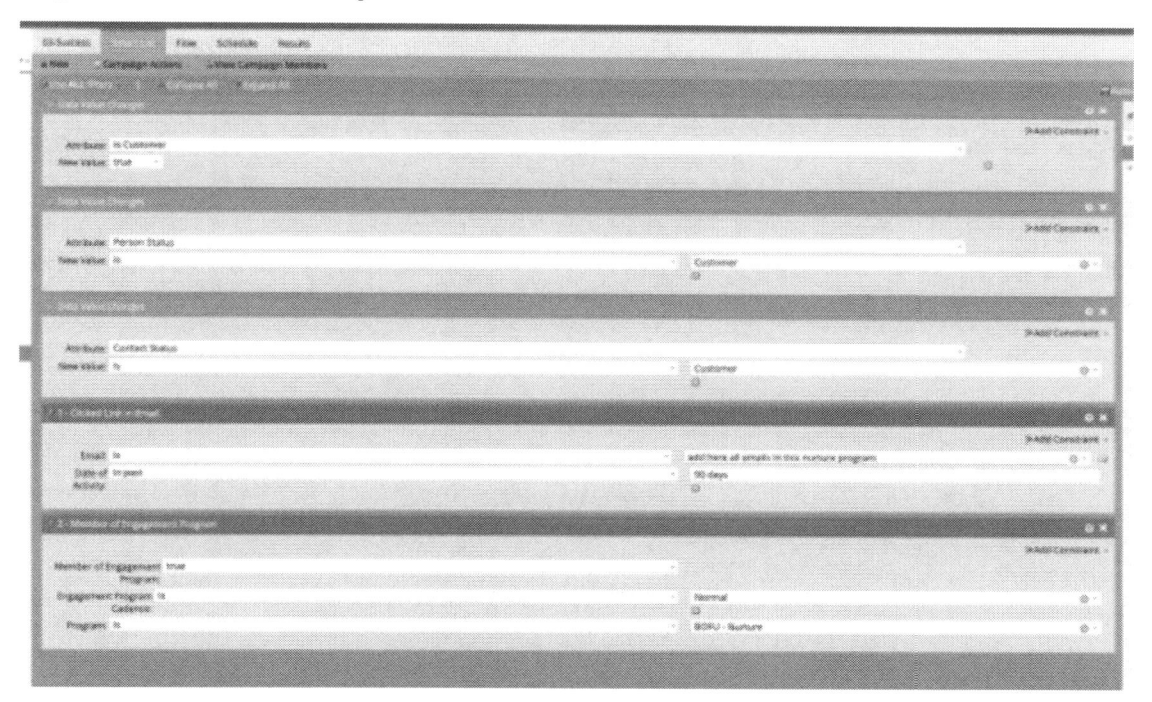

Once you have added your required logic, proceed to the flow tab:

Flow Tab Criteria:

(1) Change Program Status: to "Influenced" (or whatever status in the Nurture Channel represent success for your organization)

(2) "Add to Engagement Program" = "Customer Nurture"

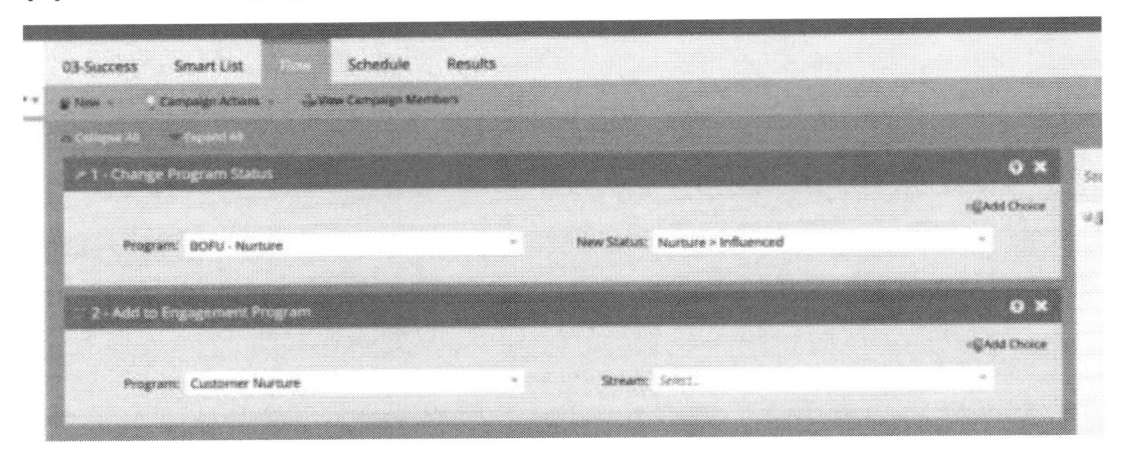

[Screenshot showing Marketo smart campaign flow with:
- 1 - Change Program Status: Program: BOFU - Nurture, New Status: Nurture > Influenced
- 2 - Add to Engagement Program: Program: Customer Nurture, Stream: Select...]

The next types of recommended nurture programs a prospect can move into can vary from one organization to another. Below are some example ideas of best-practice nurture programs that can be easily built and customized as needed to ensure that your organization is nurturing every type of prospect, or customer, from one end of the funnel to the other!

Please note that the same level of configuration detail as above is not provided below, but hopefully using the frame-work from the above campaign examples, and your knowledge of setting up smart-campaigns in Marketo, the examples below should be relatively painless to build out. The below examples are captured from working with various types of organizations and narrowing them down to two that are relevant for most organizations. Again, I place emphasis and the importance of customization and personalization for your specific organization to ensure campaign-logic is tailored as specifically as possible. The below examples should be used as a frame-work to build upon at the very minimum. Now, let's start with the first example, and an obvious transition from the BOFU-Nurture program.

Customer Nurture

The first example that we'll discuss is a customer nurture and conceptually the configuration should focus on your customers. Custom CRM fields used to indicate if accounts are customers can be easily leveraged in the same type of campaign structure. For example, in the customer nurture "**01-Add to Nurture**" smart-campaign, you'll want to use a field such as "Is Customer" and a Trigger that ensures they were part of an opportunity that was moved into the stage of "Closed Won", or similar stages in CRM. The content for this type of nurture should primarily focus either on what new customers have purchased to increase adoption, onboard successfully, help avoid common pitfalls, or attempt to up-sell or cross-sell. There are various ways to personalize each stream for customers as well. If you have multiple product lines, each stream can cater by product. If you have Enterprise accounts that you would consider "Tier 1" or the most lucrative for your business overall, you may consider a stream that applies dynamic content (discussed in an earlier chapter) to personalize the content for each organization (for example display the logo of the prospect's company who is reading the email) to increase retention. Regardless of your strategy to market to customers, this type of nurture program is usually a **must-have** for all organizations.

Opportunity-"Closed-Lost"-Reason-Captured Nurture

Our next best-practice nurture program that's fundamental in ensuring you're increasing your success with engaging as many different types of prospects as possible, are those who have had a "closed-lost" opportunity. It's a true, yet sad, part of any organization to have closed-lost business. There's no way around it. But there are ways to minimize the impact and increase the probability to win some of them back at a later point in time. **The key to this nurture program is to ensure that you sales team is diligent with capturing a "closed-lost-reason" upon closing out the account**

in CRM. If they are not, the marketing team (and in-turn the sales team later on) will miss out on a sub-set of prospects that may potential convert to closed-won at some point in the future. A great example that I've used when working with marketing teams is using closed-lost opportunities who go with a competitor.

Let's assume your sales team has pick-list field that has this as an option (opportunity lost due to a competitor, or something similar) in CRM. In this example, you may also know that your competitor has an annual subscription. Upon moving the lead/contact to this specific closed-lost-reason in CRM, you can build a trigger smart-campaign that will add leads and contacts into this type of nurture immediately where a "wait" flow-step is applied for 9 months (or any duration that is applicable to your business). Basically, they will sit in a queue for 9 months until they proceed into the stream where they will be nurtured to showcase why your organization's value propositions outweigh those of your competitors.

The key here is to understand, and accept, that you won't get all of the closed-lost prospects back, but some are sure better than none! Again, the best practice for this type of nurture strategy starts off with your organization's data-hygiene and if you are capturing the reasons why accounts are placed in closed-lost in the first place. Organizations who offer an easy standardized pick-list for reps to choose from have the most success with scaling these types of programs. **The different types of options and reasons will be the basis for the strategy that you will build each stream for**. Using my example above, the content can be built into stream 1. Then, a second, third, fourth, and so on, pick-list option for why someone closed-lost can be stream 2, stream 3 and so on.

Other Types of Nurtures: Default-Program-Type Nurtures & Nested Programs

Lastly, there are times when a Marketo Engagement Type Program (represented by the small flower-pot icon) may not be the best choice to build a nurture program from. There are some caveats to be aware of before taking the time to actually build out your nurture strategy. All too often I've worked with customers who were eager to get started and began working on building out their nurture program structure only to get to the part where they are **scheduling** their emails and get stuck. The **first item** to be aware of is the limitation with the cadence that you can schedule.

Let's say you have a requirement to send out two emails in one day.

Or, you want to send your first email on day 1 at 6am, the 2nd email three days from that, and the 3rd email 7 days after the 2nd email. You will not be able to accommodate these types of custom cadence requirements with a general engagement program type in Marketo. Sending an email once per day, at the same time, will be the only option to set the cadence with this type of nurture program. To accomplish this requirement, you will need to create a **default-program-type** and build out this logic using general smart-campaigns that will accommodate a more flexible ability to add wait steps between each "Send email" flow step. Below is an example of a flow-tab that will allow you to create a nurture with multiple emails where send times vary based on your custom requirements.

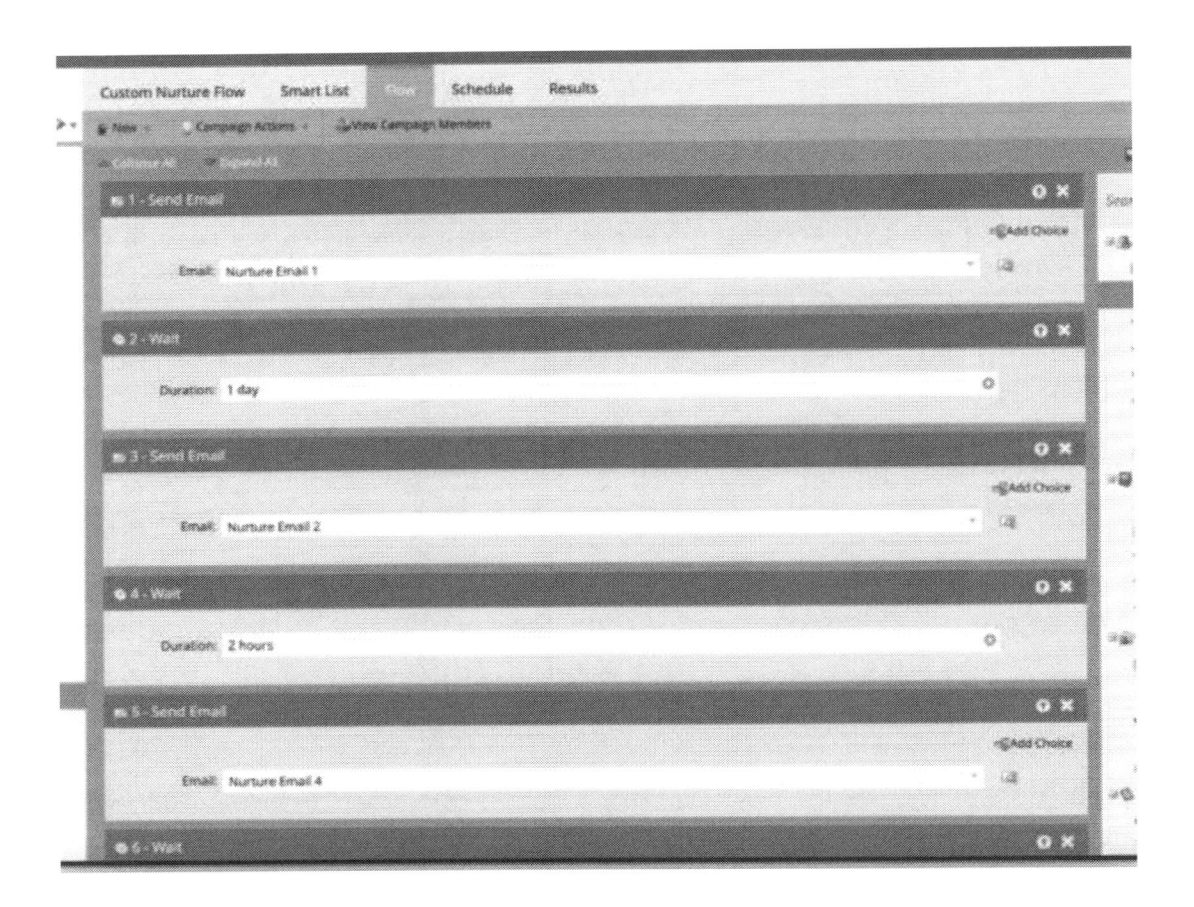

The next most commonly requested function from marketing teams I've heard for these types of nurture programs is "I have my first email sent, but after that email has been delivered I want to send email 2 to those who clicked into the first, and email 3 to those who have not clicked into the first email. Can I do that?" The answer is no, at least not with regular engagement program type (represented by the flowed icon in Marketo). Each nurture program stream in the regular engagement program type will need to wait until the cadence time is reached. Then, it will fire the next email. The nurture program will repeat that for each email in the stream unless Marketo reads that a prospect may have already received the same content prior. Marketo captures the email ID on the back-end and will auto-prevent a prospect from receiving the same email twice (unless of course it has been cloned and re-purposed).

The best way to accommodate the above type of requirement is to create multiple nested programs. When I say "nested" I mean create a completely separate **default-type**-program (represented by the folder icon) and build a single smart-campaign inside of it with the above logic. To do this, right click on the main parent-program, and select "New Local Asset". Once the popup appears, select the "Default program in the bottom left, as shown below:

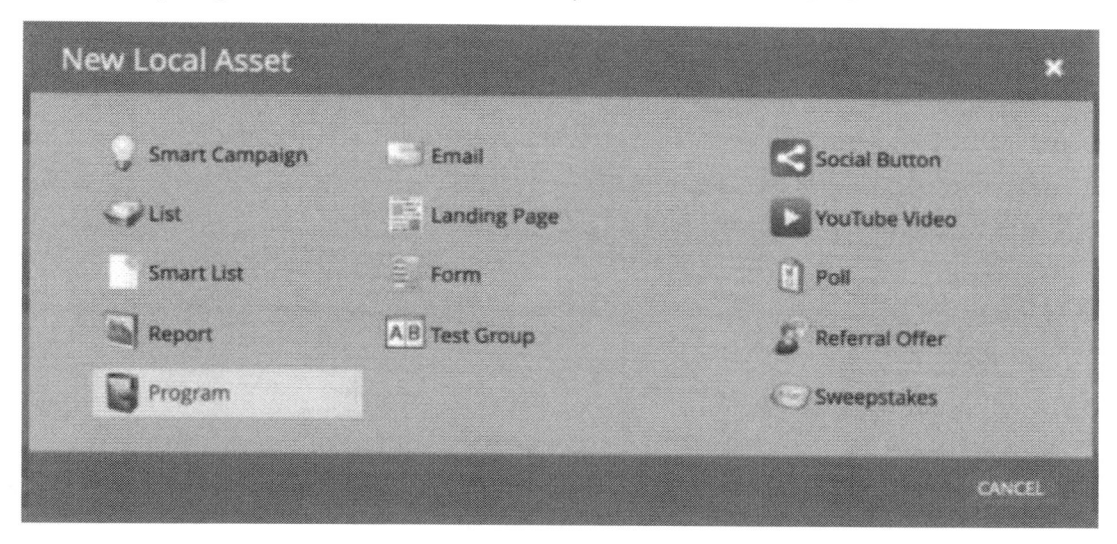

Now, create a separate sub-folder under your "Assets" folder for "Nested Programs". Remember, stay organized to ensure these are easily found in the future for any editing and/or to troubleshoot any issues within them. Then, create additional sub-folders **for each nested program** to stay organized and consistent!

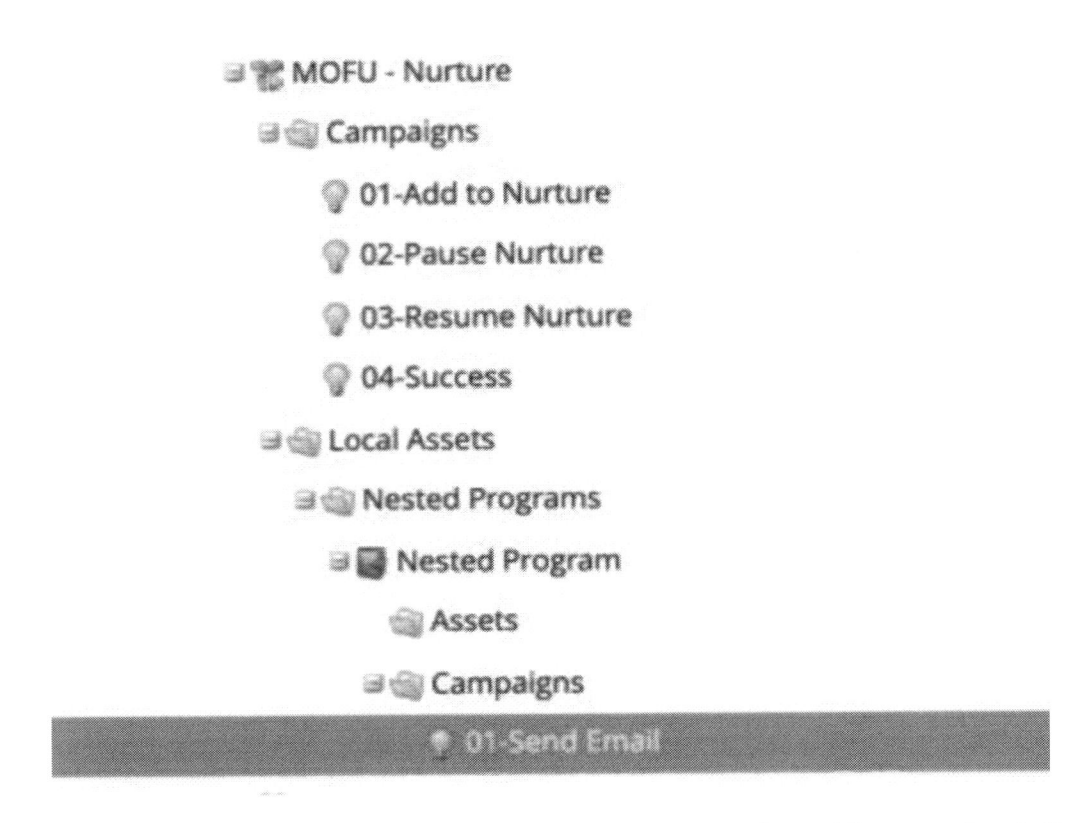

```
⊟ 🌱 MOFU - Nurture
    ⊟ 📁 Campaigns
        💡 01-Add to Nurture
        💡 02-Pause Nurture
        💡 03-Resume Nurture
        💡 04-Success
    ⊟ 📁 Local Assets
        ⊟ 📁 Nested Programs
            ⊟ 📦 Nested Program
                📁 Assets
                ⊟ 📁 Campaigns
                    💡 01-Send Email
```

Once you are ready to build the smart-campaign, it's required that you add a filter in the smart-list tab of that nurture called "**Member of Engagement Program**" and reference the main nurture-type-program that you're building this separate default-type program for. Otherwise, you will not be able to add it into the stream. Below is how the smart-list tab should appear:

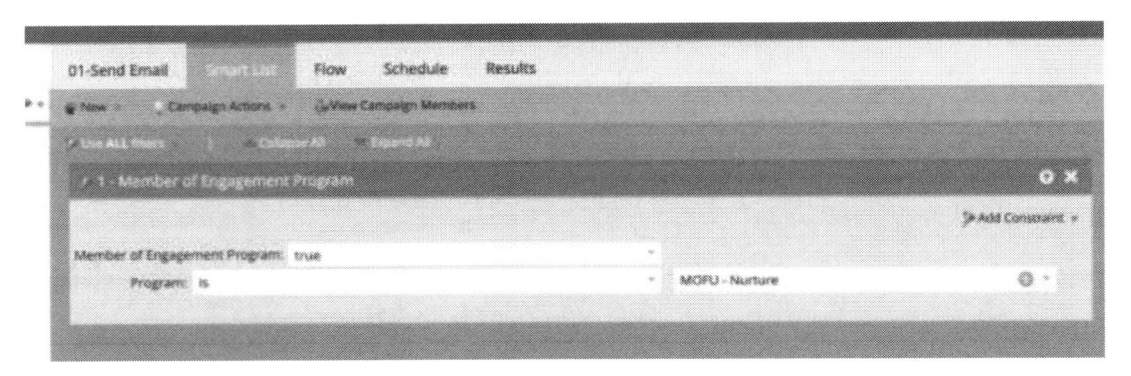

Once you configure your Smart-list tab criteria, proceed to the flow-tab where you can use a "send email" flow step with the below two add-choices.

- **Add Choice 1** = "If" "Clicked Link in Email" = "Email 1", then send Email 2

- **Add Choice 2** = "If" "**Not** Clicked Link in Email" = "Email 1", then send Email 3

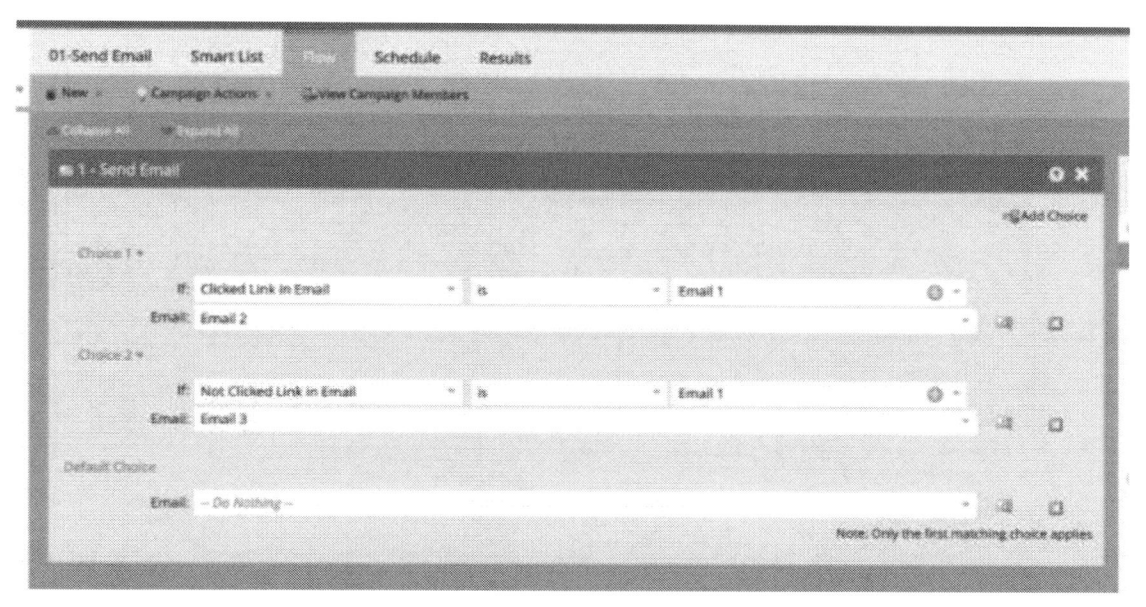

Once this separate default program is created, navigate back to your **main nurture program** and into the stream tab. Then, drag this entire default-type-nurture program into the stream it's intended for.

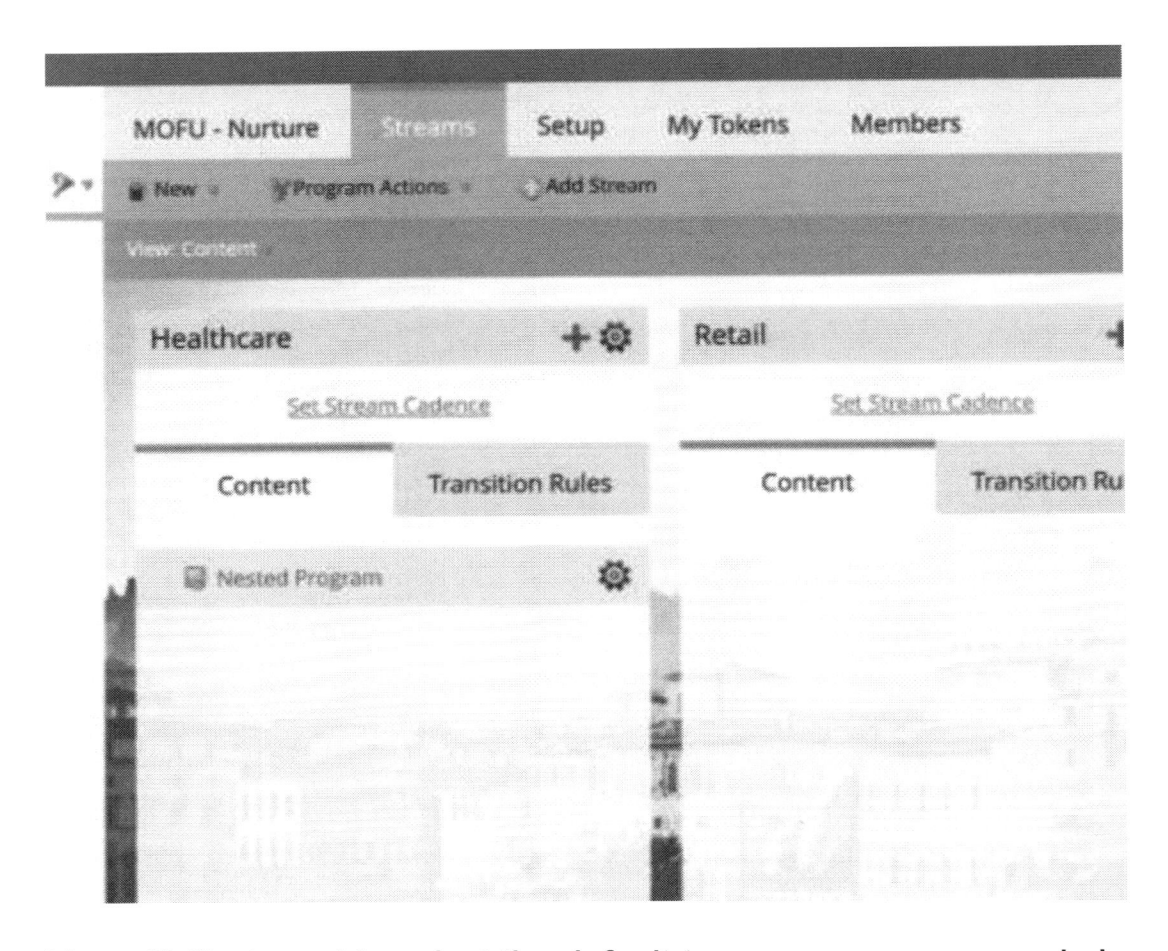

You will *first* need to select the default-type program name and also the smart campaign that has the filter for "**Member of Engagement Program**" in it to successfully nest the program here.

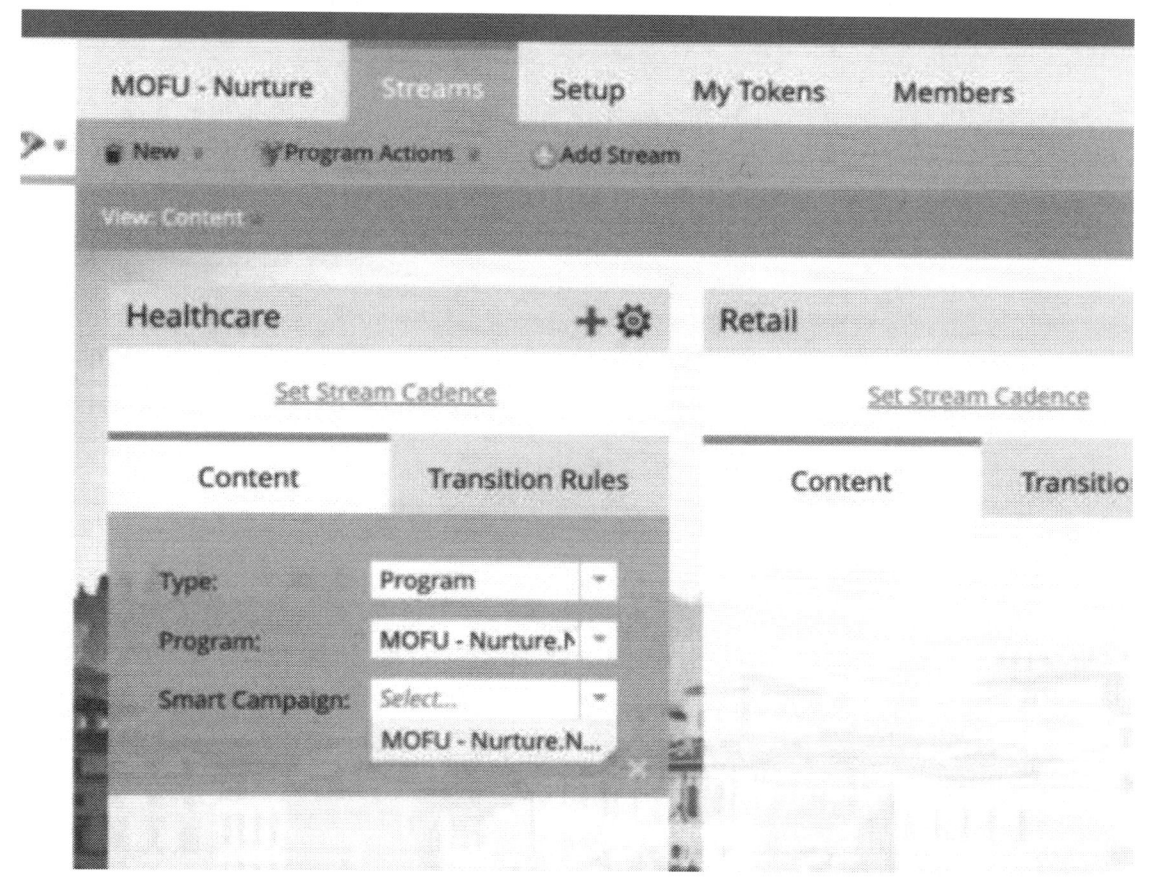

That's all there is to it! There are many other benefits for using nested programs. For example, leveraging forms and landing pages, nurturing a subset of leads/contacts that are already in the stream, adding extra flow steps to have a plethora of different ways to customize the nurture experience, and lastly to capture multi-touch attribution (which in Marketo's case is done through stamping the success status of any program). Using nested programs, you can customize and create multiple definitions of "success" for the same stream and nurture program(s).

Now that we have a better understanding of building out different nurture strategies, let's discuss how to capture all the engagement your prospects are having with your nurture emails (among ALL other types of activities) to better prioritize which prospects should be flagged for sales. In the next chapter, we'll explore lead scoring best practices, how to define your organizations Marketing Qualified Lead (or MQL) threshold, and how each scoring campaign should be setup to ensure your team is setup for success!

Chapter 4 – Lead Scoring Best Practices

As companies' scale, they'll need to become more efficient with their lead qualification process. It's impossible for organizations to follow-up on every single lead and contact that they come across. It's also not cost efficient for sales teams to shoot darts in the dark. So as companies grow, their marketing and sales teams need to be smarter about who they follow-up with to ensure their meeting internal quotas, and more importantly helping their company increase time-to-revenue!

That's why companies who purchase any marketing automation platform, such as Marketo, more often than not will setup some type of lead scoring strategy. During my consulting tenure personally, this was done for 99% of companies purchasing Marketo. Those that did not set up lead scoring in their instance are those who wasted money on a Ferrari when they really needed a station-wagon to simply email blast. There weren't many, but there were some! Don't be one of them!

If your organization owns Marketo, leverage it to its fullest capabilities, which includes having some form of a lead-scoring process. Even at its basic level, ensuring that your team is passing over relatively qualified leads and contacts to sales already saves time by not having to vet-out each prospect for basic reasons they would typically disqualify them for. For example, if your organization does not sell to students, researchers, HR or legal departments, etc., exclude these types of leads and contacts from every making it to an MQL status, and alerting sales unnecessarily. Imagine the time saved by not having to contact prospects that will never buy from your organization. Flip that on its side where you're passing over leads that are truly qualified based on known demographic and behavioral criteria you've identified and configured! Your sales team will now only work with leads they wish they had more of in the past! Now they get more sales and the marketing team gets credit for passing over strong MQLs!

Ok, hopefully you don't have to be sold the concept of lead scoring too much. If your organization is ready for a lead scoring strategy, the below best practices will ensure that you are set up for success right out of the gate! Before we jump into building anything in Marketo, I'd like to take a step back to define what "Qualified" means for your organization. I'd also like to set expectations.

Lead Scoring, or any scoring methodology is not a "set-it-and-forget-it" type of strategy. Organizations who create their scoring model and then audit, revise, and continuously optimize will find the most success with scoring. Sure, you don't need to do this daily. But, having a scoring "review" quarterly, or on some regular basis will ensure that you are still thinking about your qualified leads in a productive manner as well as optimizing any campaigns that may need a little TLC. We'll talk more about auditing your thresholds later in this chapter, but let's first discuss a starting point. Ask yourself what is important to your company that a lead or a contact must have to be considered "qualified"? What behaviors and demographics should they possess? Below is a worksheet that will allow you and your team to start mapping out exactly what's important to score on for your organization. This will make it easier to create the smart-campaigns, along with the added benefit of having an internal working doc that your team can review, update, and revise so that everyone is on the same page:

Behaviors	Score (Examples)	Frequency	Notes
Opened Emails	(+1)	Every time	
Email Clicks	(+5)	Every time	
High-Value Email Clicks	(+8)	Every time	Links that contain "pricing", etc.,
Unsubscribed	(-5)	Every time	
Visited Web Page	(+5)	Once every 2 hours	
Visited High-Value Web Page	(+8)	Once every 1 hour	Page Visits to Contact Us, Demo, Pricing, Trial, etc.,
Visited Undesirable Page	(-5)	Once every 1 hour	Visits to Careers, unsubscribe, etc.,
Visits X-number of Pages in 1 Day	(+15)	Once every 1 Day	Visits 10 web pages in 1 day
Registered for Live Event	(+5)	Every time	Fills out registration form
Attended Live Event	(+20)	Every time	Reaches attended program status
Registered for Webinar	(+5)	Every time	Fills out registration form
Attended Webinar	(+20)	Every time	Reaches attended program status
Attended Tradeshow	(+20)	Every time	Reaches attended program status
Filled Out Form	(+10)	Every time	Fills out contact-us or any other type of forms
Score Decay for No Activity	(-10)	Every 90 Days	No activity or score changes in 90 days
Downloads High Value Content	(+15)	Every time	Gated Asset Downloads for Pricing, Product, etc.,
Fills Out Demo Form	(+20)	Every time	Form titled "Demo"
Other Custom behaviors related to our org.			Any other custom behaviors relevant to your organization
Demographics	High/Mid/Low Scores	Once per Person	Read Below
Industry			
Job Title			
Company Size			
Annual Revenue			

The above internal-doc should be a starting point and is **meant to be customized**. At the very least, it can be a basic starting point from where to begin your organization's lead scoring strategy and build upon as your get more sophisticated with how you qualify people. These are the standard items that most companies typically score off of and will customize further based on their own marketing initiatives. There are, however, some best practices that should be considered.

Why Customize?

Customizing the above worksheet based on your internal marketing initiatives is key here! Start by considering all criteria and logic for when you begin building your lead scoring smart-campaigns! That will be a good start, but to truly to make this portion of Marketo specific to your organization, and of course to show your team that you're thoughtful about this configuration, it's time to think about your different forms, different gated assets, events, nurtures, webpages, ads, and everything and anything the marketing team is spending time and money on (that's tracked in Marketo of course).

Ensure that you're not treating your demo-request forms the same as you would you're unsubscribe forms. Consider your product-resource pages on your website! Should these get a higher score per visit than say your "About Us" page? Do you have events that are meant for target-accounts? Encompassing all activities that you typically see that your prospects interact with is key when building out your lead scoring strategy. Don't worry if you miss one or two. The key is to either get started and optimize from there, or to refine what's already been built with the most current behaviors your prospects engage with (if changed).

Should I score higher or lower?

This is the most common question that a lot of teams who first start with lead scoring struggle with. But it does not have to be. It's recommended to start with the most basic activity that you'd give the least weight to, for example email opens. If a prospect opens an email, let's say they get 1 point. Now what about an email click? The click shows more engagement because someone is actually taking the time to find a link so they should get a little more weight for that activity. For this example, let's say they'll get 3 points. If you start with this mindset and work your way to activities that are more indicative of buying-engagement, such as form submissions, program successes, event attendance, etc., the value you place on these activities should increase.

Now, you have the flexibility of incorporating a high-value concept to your scoring (and in-turn a low and mid-value scoring system). Let's discuss what is meant by a high, mid, and low value scoring system. Let's say someone visits your company's "About Us" page. They'll probably deserve a little less than if they were to visit your demo-request page. You'll want to be thoughtful of which activities are indicators of buying decisions here. Are people navigating to your careers page to make purchasing decisions? Probably not. We'll discuss this in a bit more detail once we cover demographic scoring examples in the smart-campaign walkthroughs below.

How to calculate your MQL threshold?

For those not familiar with what an MQL threshold is, it's the score that is reached when a lead does x-number of activities your organization deems makes them "qualified" to be passed to the sales development team. This is also the second-most-asked question I received during customer calls, and It's a fair question! The important thing to understand, and accept, is that a company's MQL threshold will differ from one to another. Organizations have different sales cycle, lead-volume requirements, quotas, and many other factors that would determine when a prospect is defined as "qualified". Remember, you aren't creating a system in Marketo that will be built out, instantly drive new revenue, and show-case you and your team as hero's who turned your company into a money-making empire once you click "activate". You're building a scoring system to qualify leads in a way that will help your organization scale and grow. You're creating automations that will help sales acquire leads from Marketing without Marketing having to sift through one lead at a time to qualify them manually. You're building this to help the revenue team, so their input and alignment is vital to the success of what you're creating. Keep these points in mind when defining your scoring methodology.

Once you and your marketing team define a rough draft of your scoring model (using the worksheet provided earlier in this chapter), the next critical component is having alignment with your sales team (and to ensure MQLs that are passed to them are good). It's recommended that you recruit the help of a sales manager who is familiar with what a good qualified lead looks like in your company. Then, walk them through what's called a "persona exercise" to help narrow down what characteristics make up a good MQL.

A "**persona exercise**" would entail you walking a sales manager through a few common scenarios that prospects may experience. This will help you gauge how high, or low to place the threshold number **from the get-go,** when you're starting off with your lead scoring strategy. This will be the best bet to start off with and prevents you from having to pick an arbitrary number and tweak as you go.

For example, let's say your first scenario is an upcoming webinar. Explain to the sales manager that you'll first send an email that gets opened (that's 1 point). They prospect will then click a link to get to the registration page (that's 3 points). They'll land on the landing page and fill out the registration form (that's 10 points), and if they actually attend the webinar (that's 20 points). That's a total of 33 points for that single event for 1 prospect. Gauge from the sales manager if that would that be enough for your sales team to have a conversation with that given prospect, or would they want that lead to be nurtured a little more?

Asking the right questions and understanding how your sales team is vetting prospects is vital to the success of this scoring system. The good thing is that you don't need to get it right the first time around. In fact, companies rarely do. Again, it's those who reevaluate, revise, and optimize that find the most success and provide game-changing processes for their organizations. Schedule some time with a sales manager and walk through the above exercise at least one time. Don't take my word for it...you'll see for yourself how valuable their input is for any scoring processes to work. Now that we've talked about a few best practices you should be following, let's discuss creating the actual scoring smart-campaigns in Marketo.

Lead Scoring Program(s)

Whether you're setting up a program from scratch our customizing Marketo's out-of-the-box pre-seeded programs and campaigns for scoring, you'll want to ensure their following the below best practices! As we dive deeper, you'll learn why it's important to ensure these best practices are implemented and incorporated into your new or current scoring strategy.

After you have a general idea of lead scoring smart-campaigns, you'll be creating your campaigns using the scoring worksheet (discussed earlier in this chapter) along with any customizations you've added. Since the scoring program(s), yes there can be multiple, aren't themselves marketing-to-prospects, they should be built in your "Operational folder" (**Discussed in Chapter 1**).

- Use the below **steps** and concepts when creating & modifying your scoring programs.

Step 1:

a. Navigate into Marketo > Admin > Field Management.

b. On the far-right side, **search** for two separate fields to ensure they are either present in your Marketo instance. Or, you need to create them.

c. The fields to search for are "**Behavior Score**" & "**Demographic Score**".

   i. If they are not there, create them.

   ii. To create them, select "**Field Actions**" toward the top of the screen and click on "**New Custom Field**".

   iii. When the pop-up appears, select "**Score**" as the type for each.

   iv. Once created. Proceed to step 2 below.

Step 2: Navigate to Marketing Activities > Operational Folder

Step 3: Right-click on your "Operational Folder" and create a new sub-folder called "Scoring" – (Feel free to customize the name based on different custom scoring strategies. For example, you may want to create different scores for different products, business units, etc., To do this, you'll want separate custom Marketo scoring fields (type=score) to ensure you can report and score separately.

Step 4:

Behavioral Scoring

a. Right-click on the new sub-folder and select "**New Program**".

b. Name the Program "**Behavior Scoring**"

a. Set the Channel to "**Operational**" when the popup appears.

b. The program type should be "**Default**".

c. Once created, right click on the new program & Select "Clone".

d. For the 2nd program, name it "Demographic Scoring" and set the channel to "Operational" as well.

Step 6: Now, right-click on the "Behavior Scoring" program and select "New Smart Campaign"

**PLEASE NOTE: - This will be the first campaign that you are building and the only example we will use. It is recommended that you use the same exact concepts and configuration for all of your remaining scoring campaigns that you will be building out. Again, the concepts and how the smart-campaigns are built will be the same throughout all of your behaviors smart-campaigns. The demographic campaigns will be slightly different and discussed further in this chapter.

To begin, let's use the example in your worksheet for Email Clicks.
   a.   Name your new smart-campaign "Email Clicks"
   b.   Follow all instructions below for each section of your scoring program and smart-campaigns.

Smart List Tab Criteria:

(1) Trigger: Clicks Link in Email = "Is Any" (Open the drop down (or operator) next to the word "Email" and select "Is Any").

The reason you'll want to consider "is Any" for this setup is to ensure your scoring campaigns are scalable. Unless you have specific emails that you may want to give more or less weight to, using this specific operator will prevent you from having to come into this campaign and add or remove emails in the future.

Flow Tab Criteria:

(1) (Change Score) – The score name is "**Behavior Score**"

(2) (Change Score) – The score name is "**Person Score**"

The reason you need two flow steps here is one will be used for the behavior score field (which tracks individual behaviors and adds them up separate from the demographic score), and the second is for the total "person score" (which is behavior + the demographic score). Having two separate score fields for both demographic and behaviors scoring allows you to measure how good, or bad, of a demographic or behaviors fit any lead is. But basically, what will happen is once the behavior score is stamped on the person record, the same score is simply added to their overall person-score field.

Now, to add the score amount on the right side of the flow step, we'll want to use **program tokens**. If you've never used program tokens or are asking why you should use them, the reason is it will be much easier for you to manage these scoring programs using tokens versus adding direct scores into these flow steps, such as a value of +5.

Just so it's clear, DO NOT add a number, such as the below "+5" into the flow step:

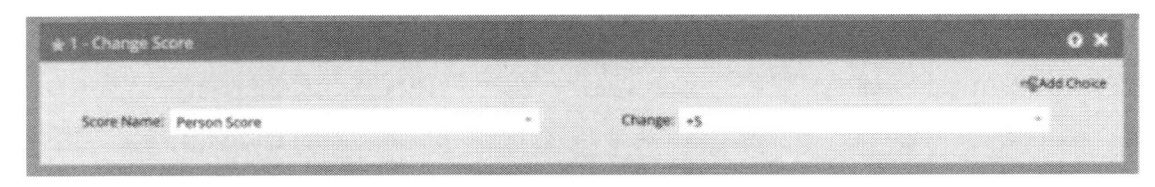

I'll now explain what you **SHOULD DO**, and more importantly why you should do it!

To create a program token,

    a.   Navigate back to the program-level of the "**Behavior Scoring**" program

    b.   Select the "**My Tokens**" Tab.

    c.   Drag over the "**Score**" token into the center:

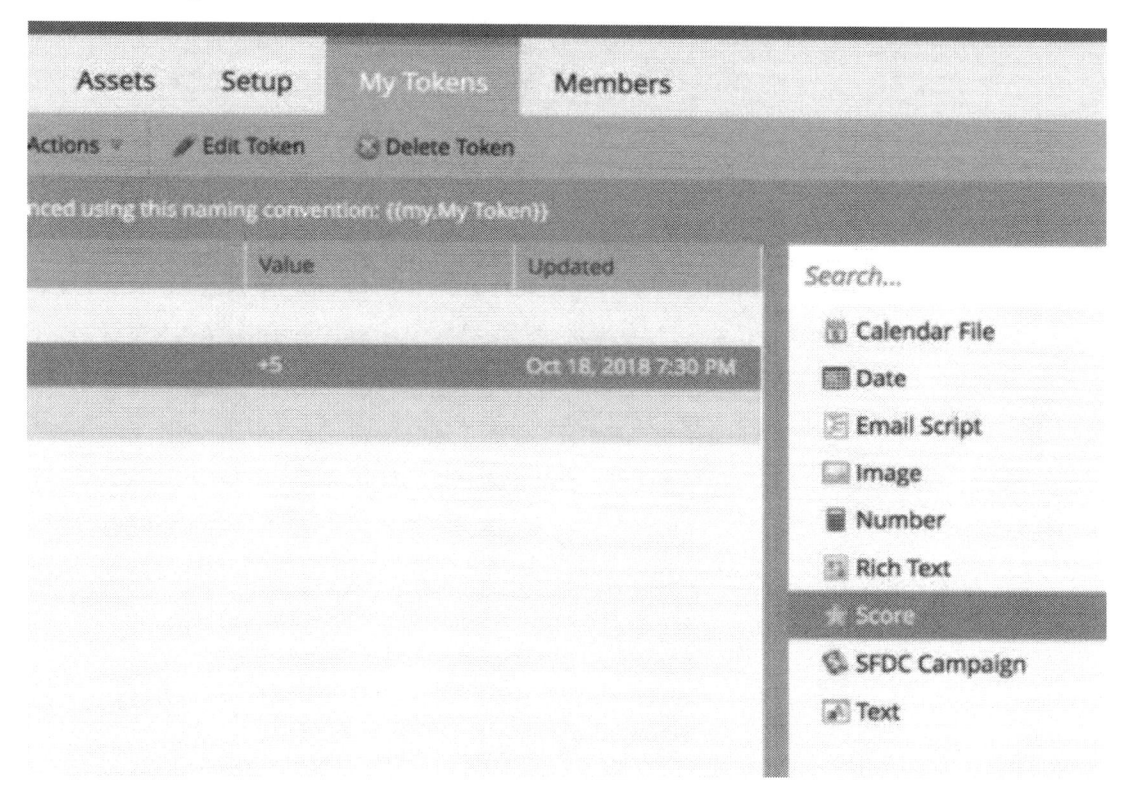

    d.   **Best Practice** - Name the Token the same **exact** name as the smart-campaign so that you know where that token will live in the event you need to make modifications later on or adjust the score amount.

    e.   Once you added the name, on the right-side add the value you want to either positively score or negatively score for the behavior it will be used for. In this example for email clicks, will use **+5**.

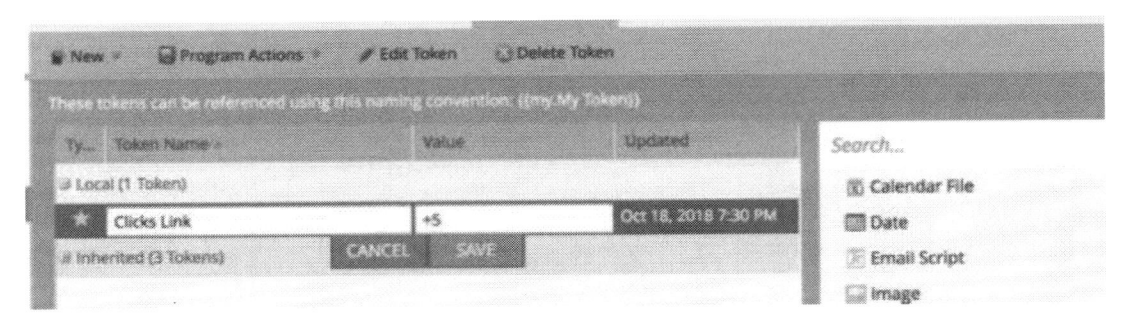

f. Once completed, click **Save** and then hover over the name/title of the token again

g. Then, click on the name so that it highlights.

h. Copy the name of the token so that you can paste it into the smart-campaign's flow step.

i. Then once it's copied, navigate back into your smart campaign and add it into the flow tab. As shown below:

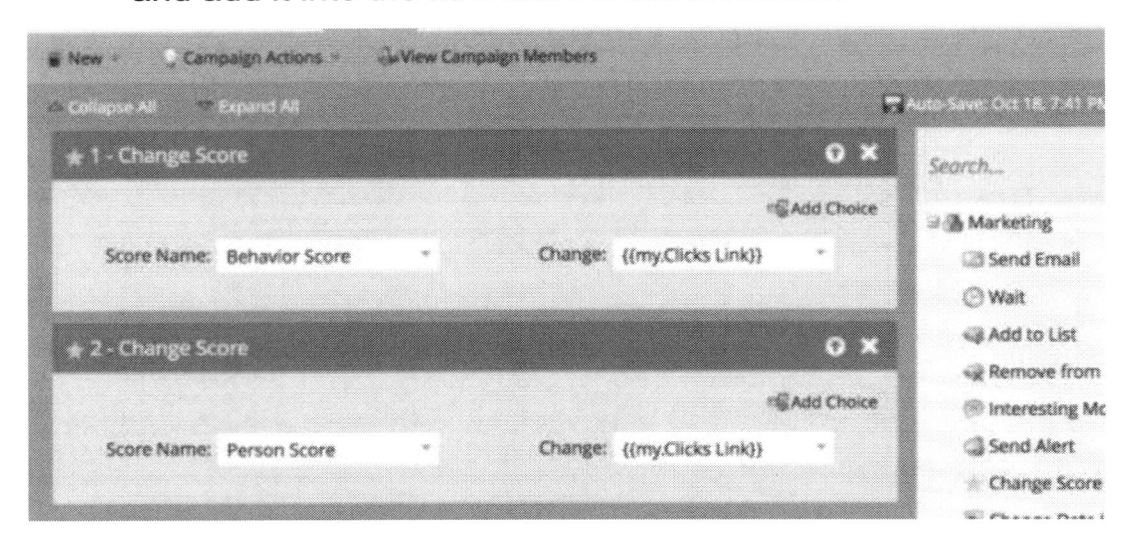

The purpose of using program tokens for each score is for **easier program management**. Consider the worksheet you have created from the previous chapter. There are probably more than 5 or 10 campaigns you will need to create so that you can score off of different behaviors that you would like to track. You will need a separate smart-campaign for each separate activity, or demographic, you are scoring on.

If you add a simple value of +5 into each flow step and decide later to make adjustments (which you should when needed) it will be a hassle and headache to have to jump around from one campaign to another, changing out scores, and having to recall where each modification was made when dealing with large sets of campaigns. Having all the scores live in the "My Tokens" tab of the parent-program allows you and everyone on your team to easily manage the scores on a **single one-page view**. You can also make changes to the scores directly from that single-one-page view and automatically push them into any of their respective smart-campaign flow steps that they reside in. This saves you a TON of time and keeps everything clean, organized, and in one central place!

PLEASE NOTE: Replicate the same steps used for this smart campaign for the rest of your behavior-related smart-campaigns. Now, let's jump into **demographic scoring.

Demographic Scoring

Before we proceed, remember that you should have already cloned a "Demographic Scoring" program. To make your life even easier, simply:

a. Clone any behavioral-scoring smart campaign into the "Demographic Scoring" Program, so that you can simply edit it without having to build from scratch.

b. When the popup to clone appears, name the new cloned smart-campaign with the title "**Industry**" (if in fact Industry is a demographic you would like to score on).
a. We'll use industry (or vertical) for this example

Once the campaign is clone, click into the smart-list tab and follow the below configuration:

Smart List Tab Criteria:

(1) Filter: Industry - and set the operator to be "**Not empty**"

The reason we have the operator to "Not Empty" is to only score records that have the "Industry" field populated. Ensure you have this field on your acquisition forms, or as a mandatory field in CRM to ensure records are getting scored appropriately in this campaign. The same applies to all other fields related to demographics that you'd like to score on. Marketo won't know to apply a score if that field is blank for someone.

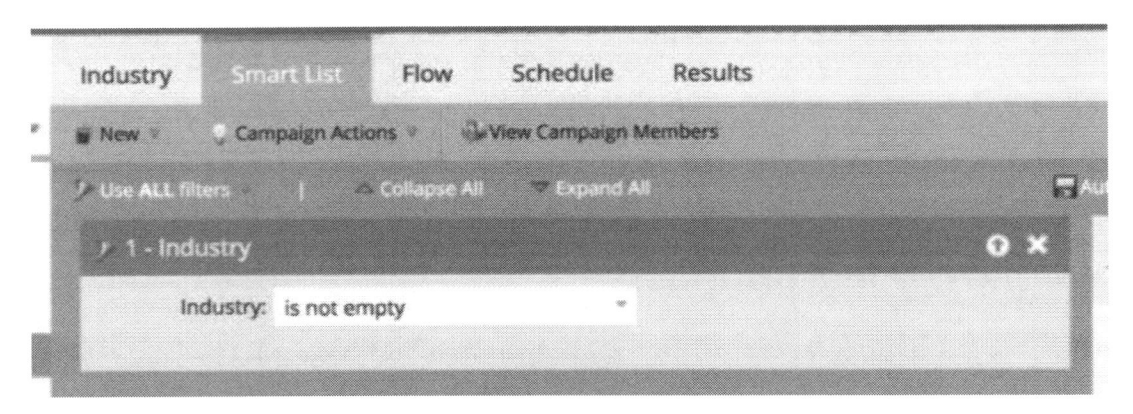

Flow Tab Criteria:

(1) (Change Score) – The score name is "Demographic Score"

(2) (Change Score) – The score name is "Person Score"

Change the above flow step from pointing to the behavior score. Instead, point it to the "Demographic Score" field. Lastly, **DELETE** the previous behavior token that you used prior to cloning this campaign. It should resemble the below screenshot if done correctly:

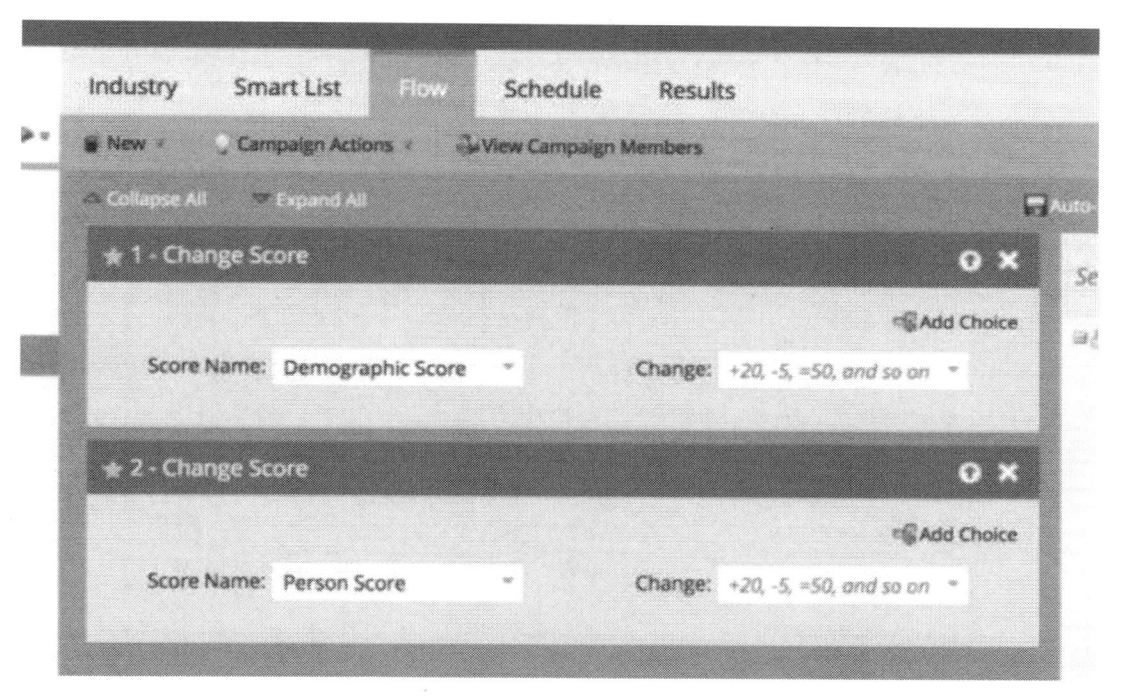

Before you begin adding tokens for different industries your organization markets and sells to, the best practice for your demographic scoring campaigns is to think of industries in a high/mid/low tiering structure. Ask yourself, what are the top industries that make up the majority of our customers? Is there just one, or are there multiple? These top-industries should be noted in your worksheet.

How about those that aren't the top ones, but also ones you sell into? What about every other industry that does not make the list? You'll have the ability to give scores to records in a scalable way depending on the different values that will populate their industry field. To set this up, you will need to:

- **(1)** Click "Add Choice" in the top right corner of each flow step.
- **(2)** Click "Add Choice" three times to create 3 rules in each flow step (for a high/mid/low value tiering structure). Your flow-tab should look like the following:

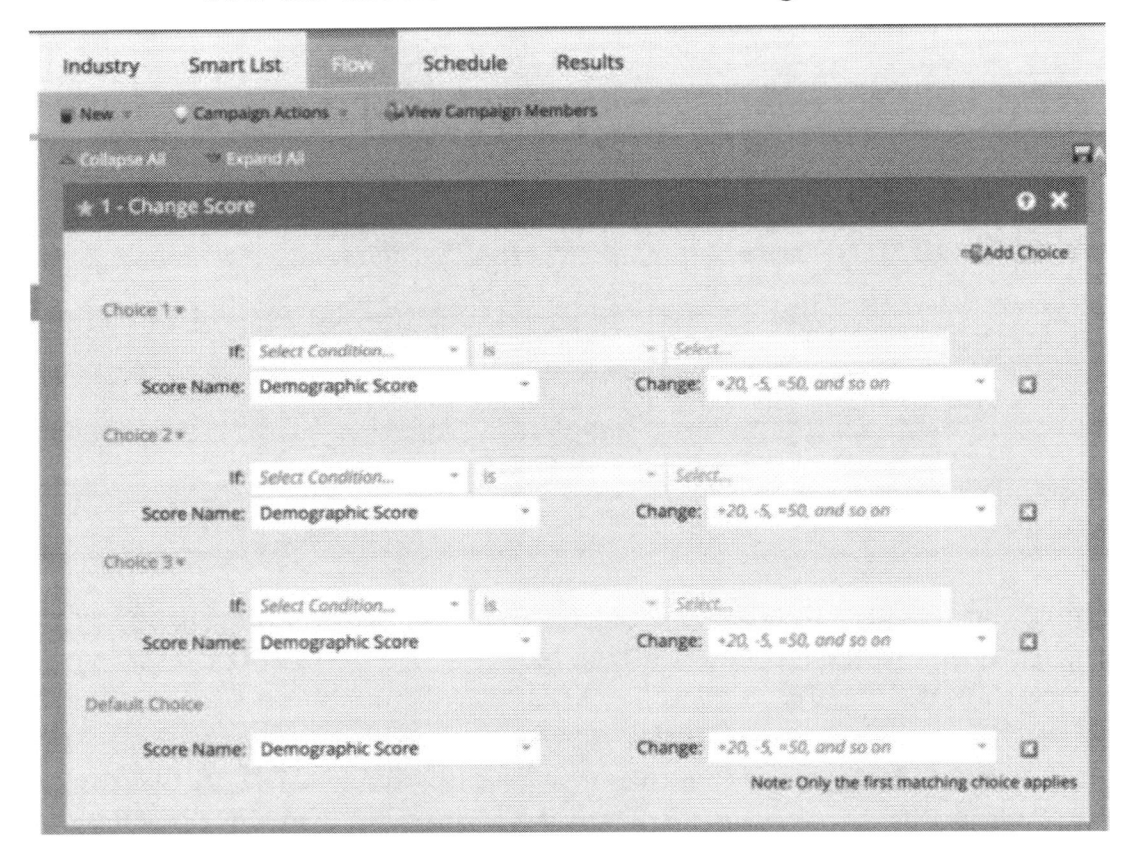

- **(3)** In each choice, **select the condition** to be set for the "Industry" field, or however your organization tracks what industry a record belongs to. (For example, some companies use a customs field to track people by vertical).

- **(4)** Then, change the operator for all of the choices to "**Contains**".

- **(5)** Before we begin adding the actual industry values and scores, by using three add-choices in this flow step we are designating the top choice for your **high-value** industries, the middle choice for your **mid-value** industries, and the bottom choice for every other industry you'd like to give the smallest score to.

- **(6)** Now, in the "**Select**" drop down, add the industry values that make up each tier. In the example below, I will use two for each tier. For example, in my organization the top industries that make up most of our customers are **manufacturing** and **forestry**. For the mid-tier values, or those industries that my organization sells to but that make up less of our customer base are **automotive** & **retail**. Lastly, for the low-value tier, these include every other potential industry that we sell into, such as **gaming** and **insurance**. The configuration for this flow tab should look like the following:

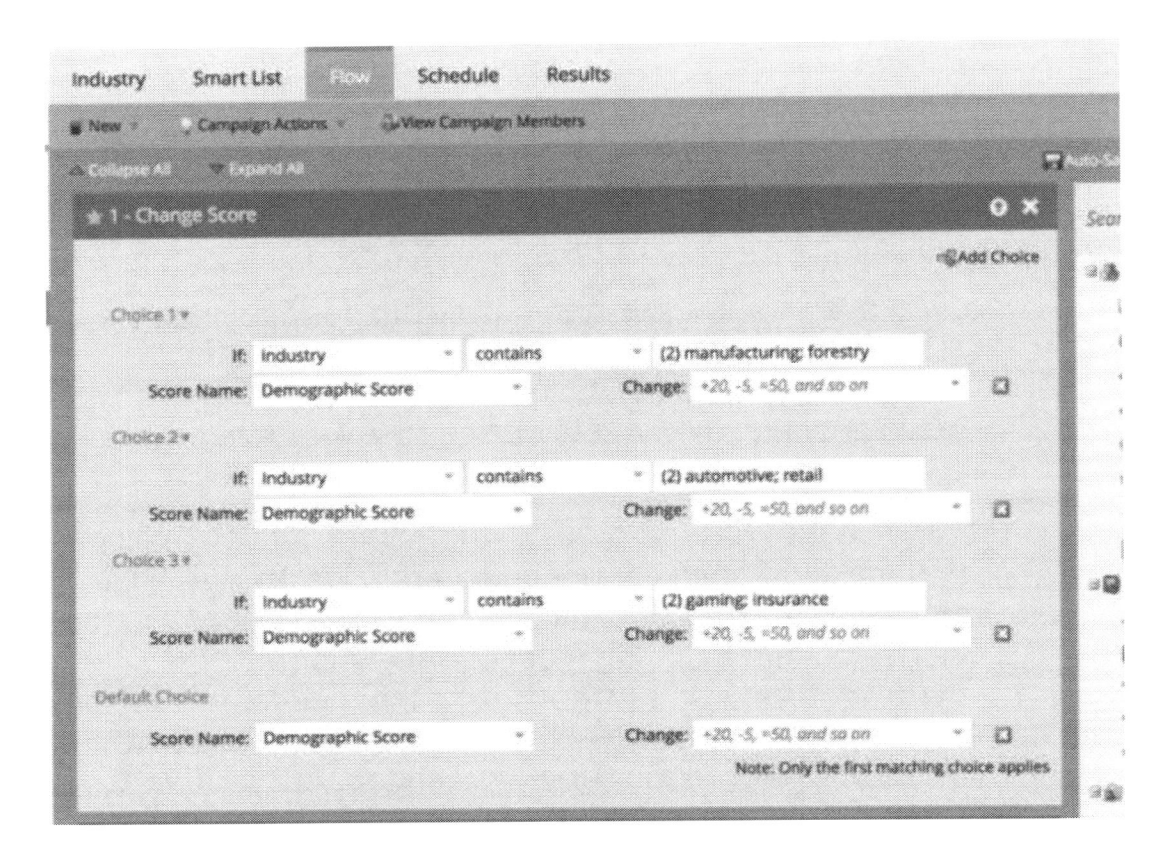

You'll need to create tokens for **each of the choices** you've made, which is simple! Again, you'll need to:

   a. Navigate back to the program-level of the "**Demographic Scoring**" program

   b. Select the "**My Tokens**" tab

   c. This time you will create three tokens, or one token for **each** tier that you've made.

   d. Drag over the "**Score**" token into the center

   e. Name each token "**Industry – High**", "**Industry – Mid**" & "**Industry – Low**"

f. Give each token a score that resembles the weight and value you place on each, for example "+10", "+6" and "+3", respectively.

The "**My Tokens**" tab with the new tokens should look like the following:

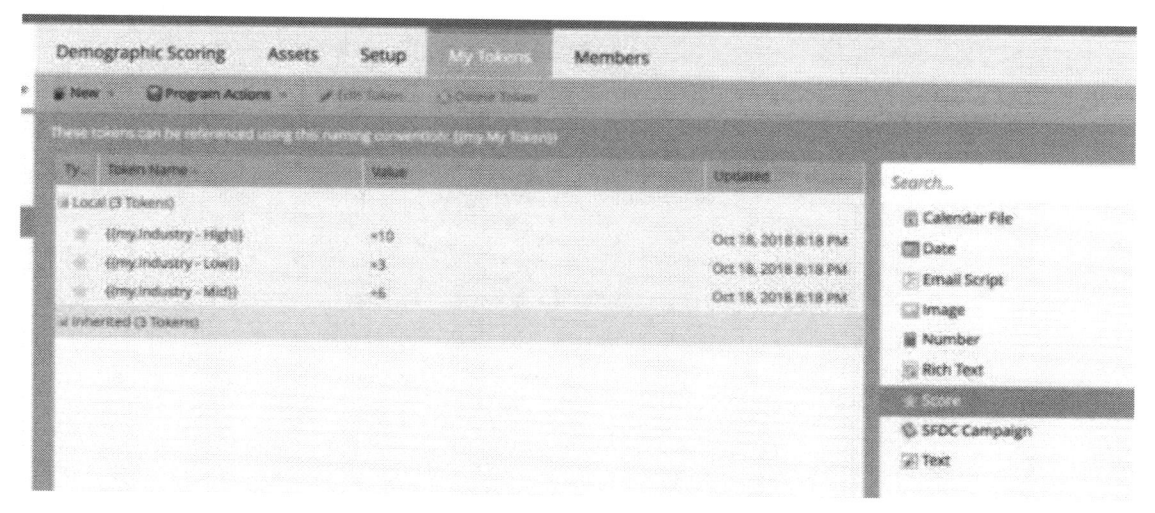

![My Tokens tab screenshot showing Local (3 Tokens): {{my.Industry - High}} +10, {{my.Industry - Low}} +3, {{my.Industry - Mid}} +6, all updated Oct 18, 2018 8:18 PM]

a. Now, **copy and paste** each token **in each flow-step add-choice**. You can do this by clicking it once, and when the token name is highlighted, right-click and select copy.

b. Then, **navigate back** into the Industry smart-campaign and select the flow-tab. **Paste each token** into **each add-choice** where it's applicable:

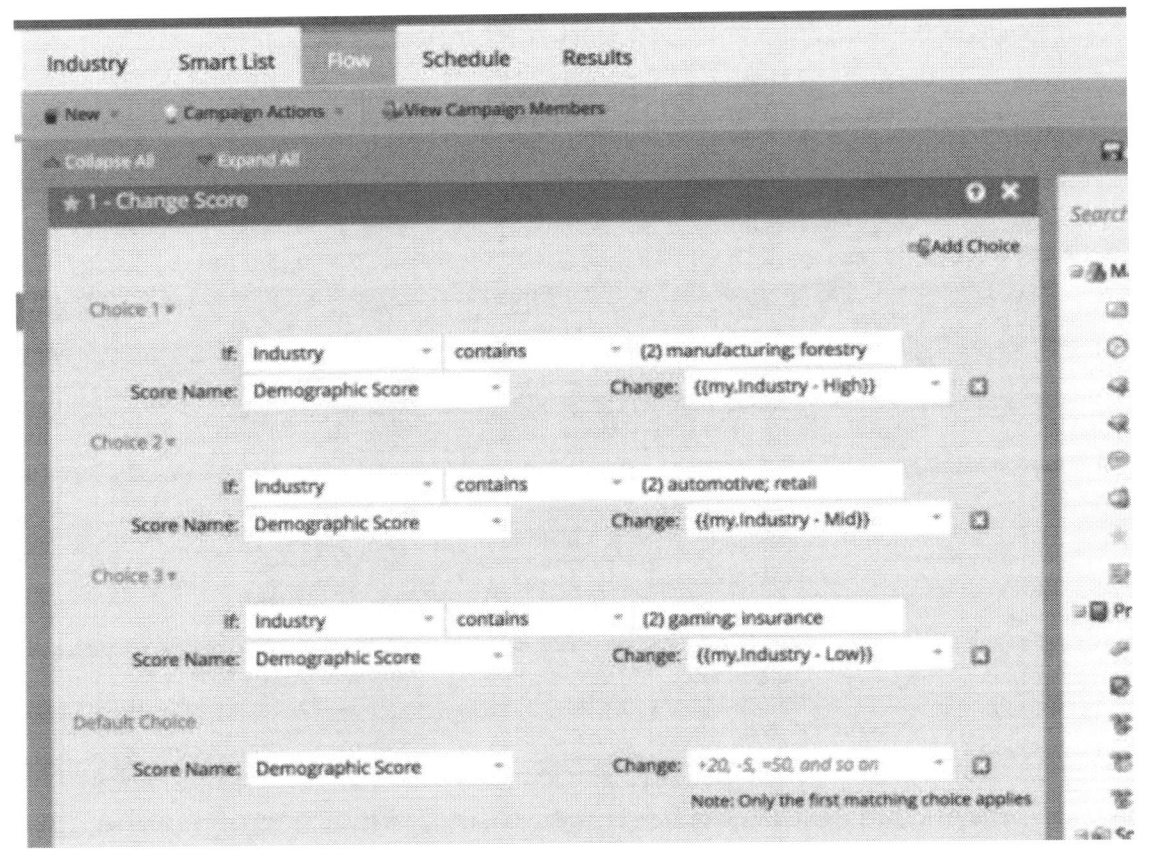

[Screenshot of a "1 - Change Score" flow step configuration with the following content:]

Choice 1
- If: Industry contains (2) manufacturing; forestry
- Score Name: Demographic Score Change: {{my.Industry - High}}

Choice 2
- If: Industry contains (2) automotive; retail
- Score Name: Demographic Score Change: {{my.Industry - Mid}}

Choice 3
- If: Industry contains (2) gaming; insurance
- Score Name: Demographic Score Change: {{my.Industry - Low}}

Default Choice
- Score Name: Demographic Score Change: +20, -5, =50, and so on

Note: Only the first matching choice applies

c. The last step for the flow-tab in the "Industry" smart campaign is to **replicate the exact same configuration you made for the top flow step**, for what was used for the demographic score field, and doing the exact same for the 2nd flow step dedicated to the "Person Score" field.

a. This is important for your scoring strategy to ensure that you are stamping the same score to the demographic score field **as well as the total person-score field** to ensure that it's adding up both demographic and behaviors scores.

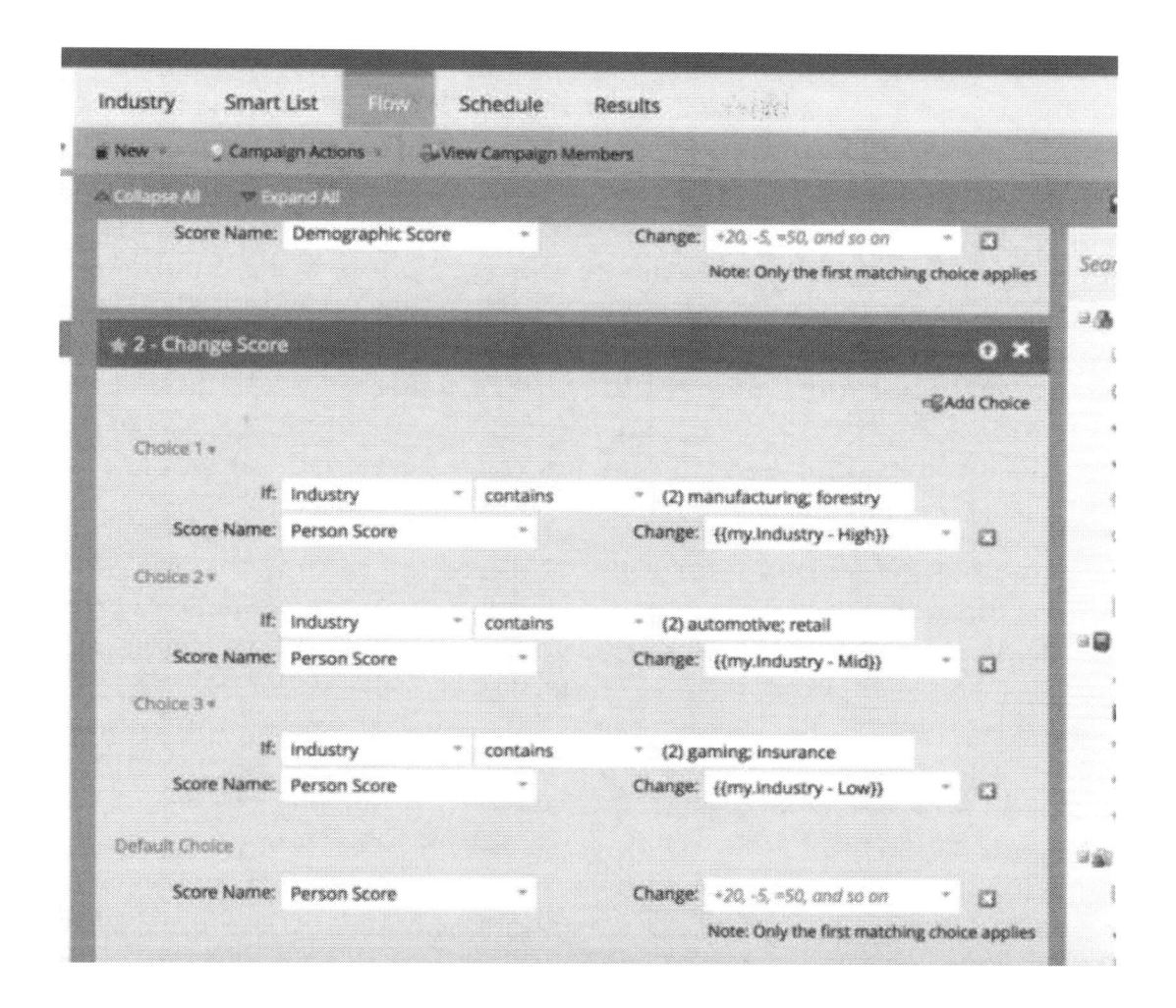

Schedule Tab Criteria:

For all of you smart-campaigns, you'll need to set a schedule.

a. Click on the "**Schedule**" Tab of your "**Industry**" smart-campaign.

b. Here, you can manage how many times each person can run through each campaign. This will differ based on what activity they are taking and how often you want to score it. For example:

For your **demographic** smart-campaigns: - The best practice is to set these campaigns to be **recurring** and run once or twice per week at a late-night hour, for example 3 am. This way, they will not conflict with any other marketing campaigns you have running during the day, which are likely more important. Also, most leads won't have their demographic fields changed often. Take someone's industry for example. Most folks won't have their Industry field changed unless they change jobs or update that field on a different form, and if your forms are set to "pre-fill" values, they'll most likely leave the value that as previously filled in. It's recommended to allow leads to run through these campaigns once every 1-2 per week, just to double-check if any changes occurred.

For your **behavioral** campaigns: - The amount of times a prospect can run through these campaigns will vary based on the activity they are taking, and how it's associated to your business and marketing efforts. For example, for event-attendance you'll probably want to score a high amount of points every time someone goes through an event program and has their program status set to "Attended" (or whatever the success-status is for that program). Realistically speaking, most prospects won't go to all of your events so when they attend one or two, this shows a great amount of engagement and is indicative of buying, so you should score accordingly! What about web-page visits? You'll probably not want to over-inflate your prospects score by scoring every single time they visit any web-page. The best-practice there is to spread the score out to something like once per hour. Think carefully for each behavior campaign to ensure that you're setting up your scoring so that it's reflective of what you typically see from real-life examples of your company's prospects that convert into customers. Do your real prospects (vs. students, researchers, or any other non-prospects) really visit multiple pages in a short period of time, or do they return to make more informed decisions as time progress, in the course of days or weeks perhaps?

Now, let's revisit the purpose of having both a behavior and a demographic score field. We want to be able to distinguish between how good of a demographic fit a lead is, as well as how actively, or inactively engaged they are from a behavior-standpoint. Using a single field for "Person Score" is great, but it prevents you from targeting and reporting on specific sub-groups of individuals in Marketo. It can also save your sales team some time by distinguishing whether they should chase down specific leads who may not otherwise be worthwhile. Let's go into some of these examples.

Maybe you want to create a report of all people who have a behavior score of X-amount so that you can send them specific content, target them for specific sales reps, or simply see from an engagement perspective how much of your database is actually interacting with your marketing, and if that's growing over time? Maybe you want to combine that with people who have certain demographic or firmographic traits? Let's say you have a specific product line catering to a specific vertical. How helpful would it be to break up your leads based on those who are in a particular industry and have already shown lots of engagement based on their mid-to-high behavior scores. Combine that with product-interest fields or scoring and you're now starting to tighten up your segmentation processes. The key takeaway from this is that it helps marketing teams segment lists and reports to ensure they're targeting the correct prospects for specific marketing initiatives.

From a sales-rep perspective, and if you leverage **Marketo's Sales Insights** tool, these two fields map to specific stars and flames that come out-of-the-box. To check if they do, simply **navigate to Admin > Sales Insight**, and confirm that they are mapped to the behavior and demographic fields, as shown below:

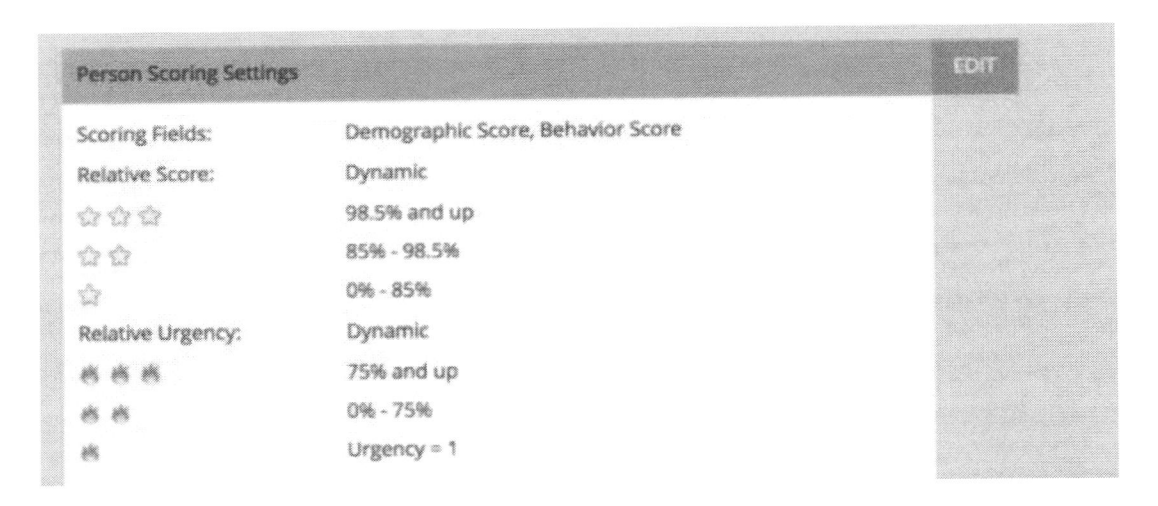

> **Person Scoring Settings**   EDIT
>
> | | |
> |---|---|
> | Scoring Fields: | Demographic Score, Behavior Score |
> | Relative Score: | Dynamic |
> | ☆ ☆ ☆ | 98.5% and up |
> | ☆ ☆ | 85% - 98.5% |
> | ☆ | 0% - 85% |
> | Relative Urgency: | Dynamic |
> | 🔥 🔥 🔥 | 75% and up |
> | 🔥 🔥 | 0% - 75% |
> | 🔥 | Urgency = 1 |

If they are not, click on the edit button and ensure the mapping looks like the following:

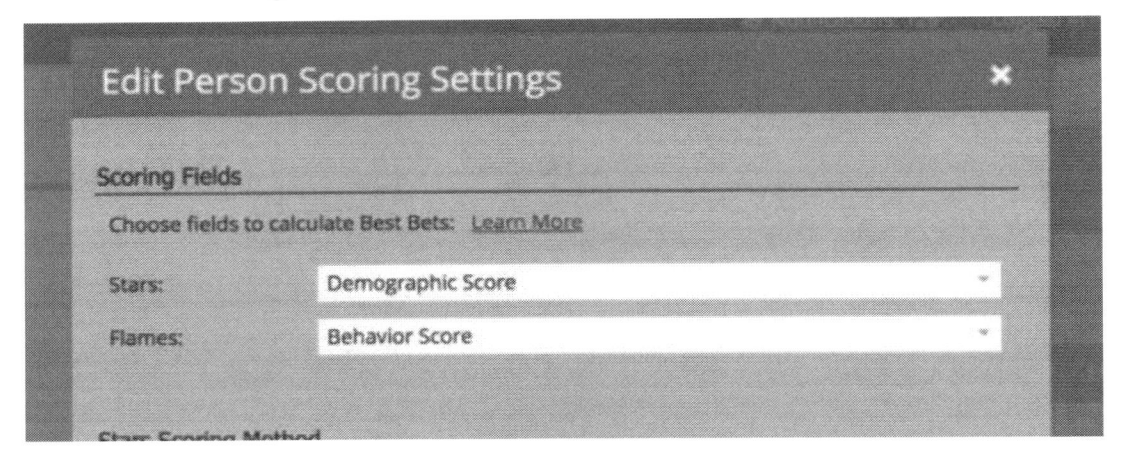

> **Edit Person Scoring Settings**
>
> **Scoring Fields**
>
> Choose fields to calculate Best Bets: Learn More
>
> Stars: [Demographic Score ▼]
>
> Flames: [Behavior Score ▼]

If you have Marketo's add-on for Sales Insights, the stars and flames appear not in Marketo, but in your CRM. They help sales reps see whether their owned leads are a good fit behaviorally and demographically! In your CRM, if a lead appears to have three **flames** next to their name, this indicates they are a great hot lead (from a behavioral-standpoint) and a sales rep should follow up as soon as possible. But, before spending time calling and chasing down leads, the sales rep can also compare the **stars** next to that leads name as well. If they see that same "hot" lead has 1 star, indicating they may be a poor demographic fit, the sales rep can drill down on that lead or contact and determine what the issue may be? Maybe that person has a job-title of "student"? Leveraging this insight will save time for sales chasing dead-end leads who may be researching your website but will never actually make a purchase. So, it's helpful to break these scoring fields out to ensure your teams have more flexibility when it comes to how you'd like to report, segment, and drill-down on prospects to make informed decisions.

Chapter 5 – PPC (Pay Per Click) Programs

When discussing the use of online ads or any kind of PPC (Pay-Per-Click) Programs, we're referring to purchasing ads via Google AdWords, Facebook, LinkedIn, and other social sites or search engines. **The concepts and configuration that we'll discuss in the following chapter is applied the same exact way to all of the different ways you are marketing with ads, and how that should be tracked inside of Marketo!** Before we jump in, it's best to start off with some fundamental concepts that is important for any marketing operations person, or really any general Marketo admin to understand before starting to create this type of program.

UTM Fields

It's a best practice to ensure that you are capturing where your ad traffic is generating from with the use of hidden UTM fields. If a prospect clicks on a hyperlink (the ad) which contains specific UTM values in the browser's URL, you will be able to see that value populate into the UTM fields that you created. That value should tell you from what add that prospect clicked on, hence giving that add credit for their traffic. You'll be able to report on which ads are performing better than others and will be able to track your investments to understand where the most ROI is coming from. Below are some examples of UTM fields that you may want to consider.

- Campaign Source: (**utm_source**)
- Campaign Medium: (**utm_medium**)
- Campaign Term: (**utm_term**)
- Campaign Name: (**utm_campaign**)

One thing to note is that you won't necessarily need to create all four fields. The above fields are simply examples for what you may like to track (in the URL) based on where the source of the traffic is generated from. We'll use the "**utm_source**" field as our example in this chapter to see how we can track different ads coming from AdWords, Facebook, and LinkedIn. If you are new to PPC programs in Marketo and have not set up any kind of utm tracking previously, I recommend starting with the same utm fields shown above in your instance and analyze the values that get stamped to understand what other data-points will be required for your specific reporting needs. But remember, it's always easy to create additional fields but you don't want to create unnecessary clutter by adding fields that won't be used.

I'll explain how this type of program will work in this chapter, but at a high-level we're adding a word, such as "AdWords" into the URL and when someone clicks the link with that word in it, and submits a form (to acquire that lead into your database), Marketo will pull the value of "AdWords" with the form submission and tie it to that lead record. This way, you know the exact source of that lead, and can even use multiple utm-values to track multiple sources, or additional data-points, from where you are creating and posting your ads. It's that simple!

Below is an example of a URL with a utm value:

Example: www.fakedomain.com/event-registration-page.html?utm_source=Adwords"

Two Different Scenarios to Consider

The next thing you should be aware of is two different scenarios that can occur once a prospect clicks on your ad. Based on these two scenarios, this will expose you to which configuration will be best for your organization's needs.

The **first** scenario is when a prospect clicks on your ad and they are redirected to a regular Marketo landing page. Landing pages are typically best practice to use since they're more personalized for the marketing initiative the ad itself was initially intended for. For prospects, it's also easier to avoid getting distracted and focus at the objective at hand! Providing a single CTA, or call-to-action, is a great way to ensure that you increase the amount of conversions on the ad you've invested in. There is also usually no site-map or additional pages on these single landing pages that leads can get distracted with and navigate away from. **This part is key**.

The **second** scenario is where you have an ad that directs your leads to your company's website. For example, let's say you've created an ad that points people to your "Contact-Us" page. When prospects navigate here, sure there will be people that convert off the form as intended. But there will also be people who will get distracted with all the other things they'll see. They may click on your "About-Us" page to read more before providing you with their information. They may look at your pricing page, solutions, resources pages, and anything else that catches their eye to divert them away from completing the form. **Once they leave the page, the UTM in the URL is instantly lost**.

Even if that prospect returns back to the "Contact-Us" page and actually fills out the form, they've already lost the UTM in the URL and you won't know the source they originated from. **This will absolutely skew your reporting and ad-cost metrics which can be a nightmare**. While the first scenario we discussed avoids this situation by not having any additional pages a prospect can navigate to and only usually has a single CTA, this second scenario is trickier.

If you feel there are use-cases where your organization will have ads pointing to your website and scenario-two is best, there are additional steps you'll want to take to ensure that you're capturing every lead's UTM-values. **This includes working with your** developer team to create a script that will be added to your website that captures the initial UTM, stores it in the event that visitor bounces off the original page (in this example the "Contact-Us" page) and appends the URM back into the URL if, and when, the prospect eventually returns to convert off of the form as originally planned.

These scripts can be built in different ways and the main concept is that the **UTM value is stored and retained** for a specific timeframe based on the person's cookie (one will need to be added to that visitor) until they eventually convert off the form. I recommend consulting with your developers to create a script like this, searching in Marketo's Community Portal for any examples that other customers possibly have shared, or leveraging unused consulting hours (or purchasing some additional time) with a technical consultant from Marketo's professional services team. The latter may be the most worthwhile to ensure time spent is efficient and testing is completed on their end. Now that we have the fundamental concepts in place, it's time to decide what's best for your organization.

**PLEASE NOTE: For the example below, we'll walk through using a simple Marketo landing page (Scenario 1) as the configuration will be identical in Marketo regardless if you are using a script on your website or a simple landing page. The same concepts will apply moving forward after you decided whether to use a script/code (Scenario 3), or whether you'll prefer to use Marketo landing pages (Scenario 1).

Step 1: (Creating UTM Fields)

To do this:

    a.   Navigate back into **Admin > Field Management**.

b. On the right-side search bar, search for any fields that may contain the word "UTM" in them.
a. If none are found, **create a new string-field named** "utm_source".
c. Now refresh the page and confirm that the field has been created.
d. Once confirmed, navigate back to **Marketo's Design Studio** section.
a. In the Design Studio, you will need to do a few things to ensure that the form and the landing page is properly setup to reflect the source of the ad's traffic. We'll first start with the form as it will need to be added to the landing page afterwards.

Step 2: (Add Hidden Field to form)

a. In Design Studio, right-click on the **Forms** option in the left-side asset tree and click "**New Form**".
b. Give it a name such as "**Ad Form**" or something similar.
c. Remember this can be a global form so if you're not going to change the fields or the CTA, you can re-purpose this form for other ads later on. If you create a local form specific to an individual or custom ad program, it's best to create it locally under that program to keep things organized.
d. Once the form is created and the form-editor has opened, add the fields you'll require prospects to fill out.
e. Once the fields have been added to the form, **add your "utm_source" field toward the bottom**.
f. Once added, on the right-side **change the field-type to "Hidden"**, as shown below:

g. Once you have selected the field type, you'll notice the option for "**Autofill**" toward the bottom of the right-side menu.

h. Click "Edit" next to it, and a popup will appear:

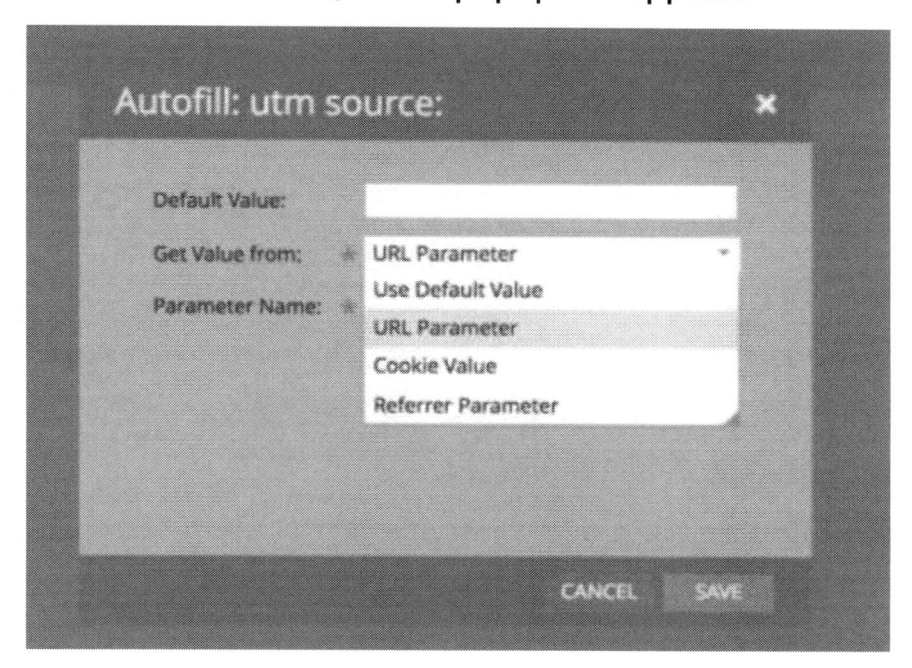

i. In the popup, expand the "**Get Value from**" picklist option and select "**URL Parameter**".

j. Once selected, you'll see an additional required option for "**Parameter Name**" appear.

k. Here, simply **type out the field name that you've created**. It should look like the following:

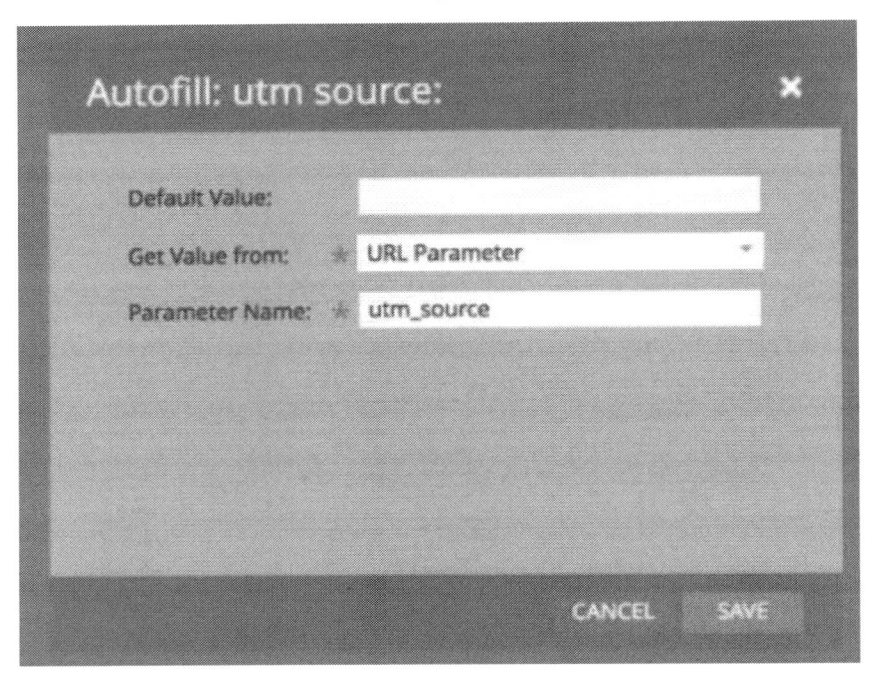

[Autofill: utm source dialog showing Default Value (blank), Get Value from: URL Parameter, Parameter Name: utm_source, with CANCEL and SAVE buttons]

l. **Click Save**, and you're all done with the form.

Step 3: (Adding the form to the landing page)

a. Once the form has been completed, **navigate to the landing page** that you will use for the ad.

b. This should be the page that prospects are directed to once they click on your ad.

c. When you've completed creating your landing page, click on "Landing Page" actions toward the top of the tab-view and select "URL Tools" and click on "URL Builder", as shown below:

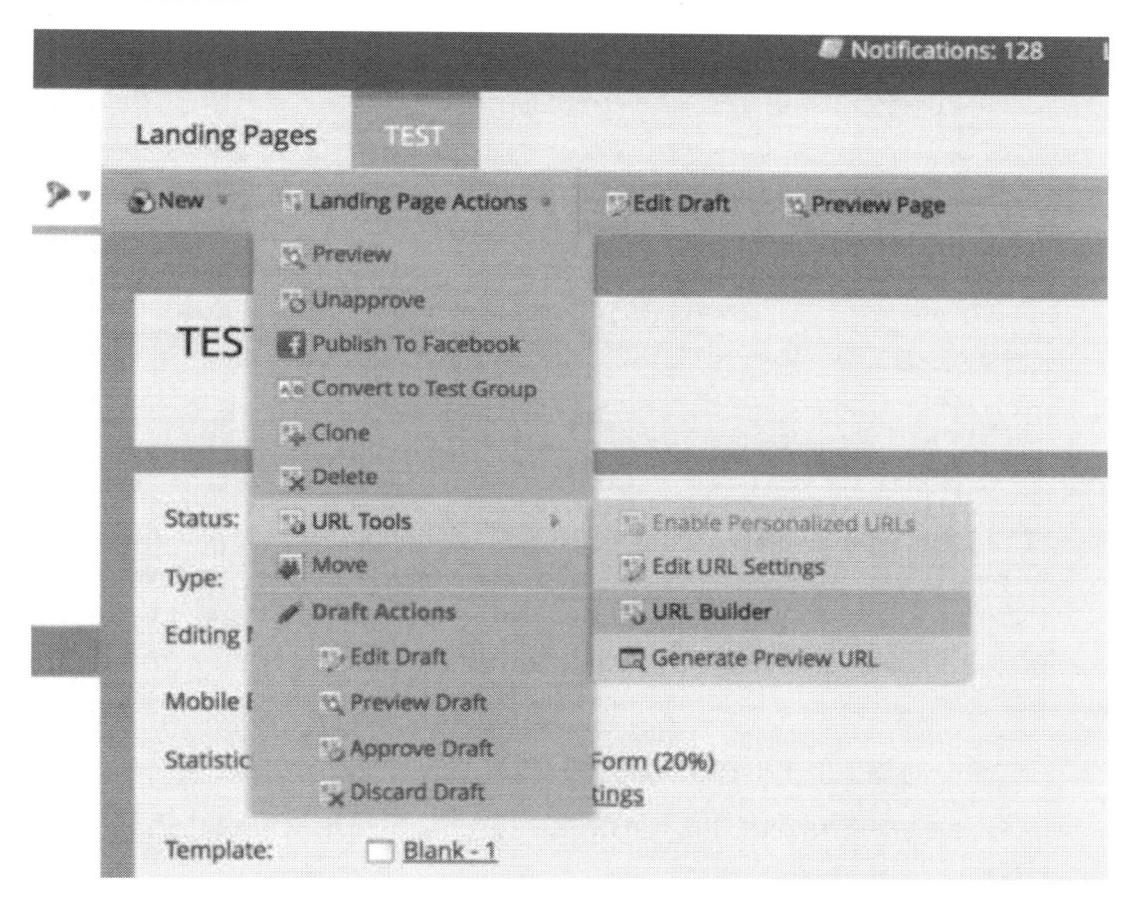

d. Once you've clicked on "**URL Builder**" a popup will appear that will allow you to customize the UTM field with a value that you'll use for your ad.

e. The popup will automatically detect any forms that are on this landing page which have any hidden fields set to "URL Parameter"

f. Ensure that your UTM field is checked and simply type in the value you would like to capture in Marketo once your form is submitted by a prospect. In this example, if you are using AdWords for your ads, type in the word "AdWords" to ensure that this value is stamped on your "utm_source" custom field every time the form is submitted on that landing page.

g. Then, click on "**Update URL**" and the bottom "Final URL" section will append the UTM parameter you've created to the URL. You will need to use this generated URL, instead of the URL generator in AdWords, for submitting your ads to AdWords, or any other search engine or social site.

Step 4: (Doing a quick Test)

Now the fun part! Using the generated URL, paste it into any browser and you should navigate to your landing page (make sure your landing page is approved). You should be directed to the landing page with the form that has the hidden UTM value one it. To test this:

(1) Fill out the form with sample data.

(2) Once you submit the form, the hidden value will instantly be collected in Marketo

(3) Navigate back into Marketo and go into the Lead **Database**

(4) In the Lead **Database** section, click on the "**All People**" system smart list

(5) **Search for the sample lead** you just created when filling out the form

(6) **Double-click** onto them for their person-record to open

(7) Navigate to the "**Info**" tab and **search for the field "utm_source"**

(8) You should see the word "AdWords" as the value on this field

The best practice here is to ensure that you have UTMs in the URLs for all the different ads that you are running and pointing to your landing pages. **This way, you can create a simple report or smart list to see how many people each ad is acquiring and how all your ads are performing (from an investment perspective).** It's that simple!

From here, you'll simply want to build your marketing programs to track separate ads individually. Add the landing pages and forms to your programs to track how each ads is converting new leads into your system.

Now that you have a much better idea of how to create a PPC or online advertising program in Marketo, let's discuss two things that most miss when starting to build these out. These aren't as obvious when you are first getting started and are usually common questions that come up later on when it may be too late to adjust, and your metrics get skewed.

The **first best practice** to be aware of here is that for each Ad you are running, you'll need **a separate program** to track it. **Secondly**, and the reason behind the first, is that you'll need **a separate period-cost**, or cost amount, for each ad to understand its value when doing your reporting later. Since Marketo allows you to only add a single period-cost to each program to track it's cost metrics, you'll want to create a separate folder to hold your separate ad programs. It's not uncommon to have dozens of programs here quarterly, if not more so don't worry about have too many of them. Remember from chapter 1, they should be getting archived later on anyway keeping your instance nice and clean.

Once your Marketo Ad program is created:

a. Navigate to the "**Setup**" tab and select "**Period Cost**" on the right side.

b. **Enter the cost-amount you invested for your ad** into the popup that appears and click Save. This will track each program's cost metrics separately to ensure that you're able to track the success of each.

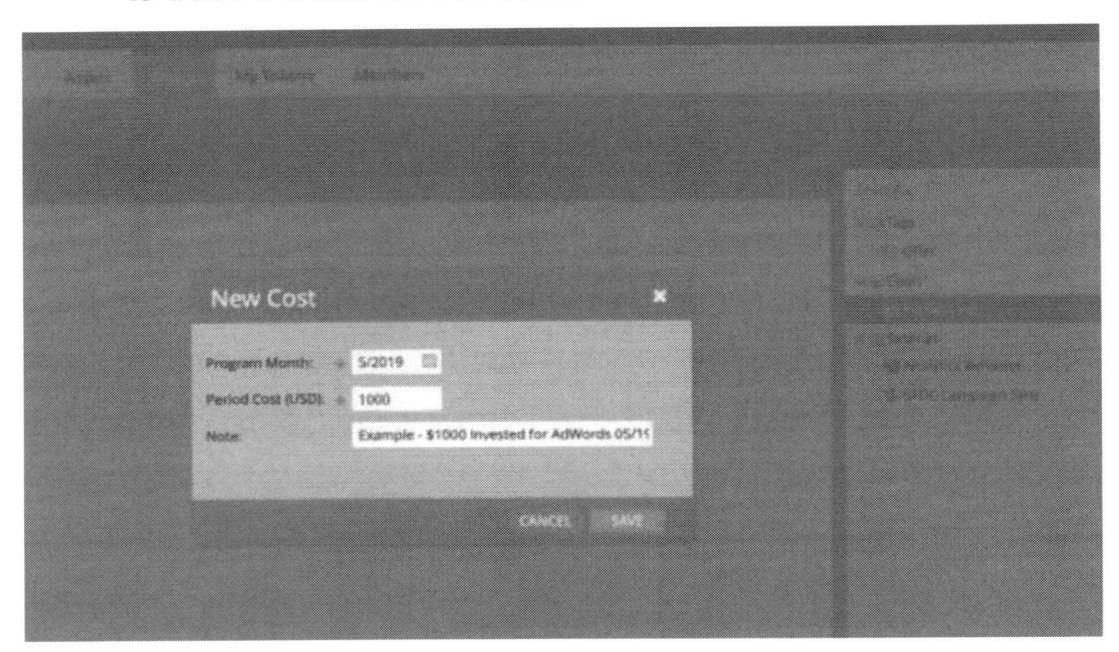

I CANNOT stress enough how important this is! Missing out on cost-metrics to ads in Marketo will mean you can't track things like cost per acquisition and cost per success, preventing you from truly measuring which ads are performing better than others. It's not enough to measure how many leads simply convert off your ad forms as you won't know what the cost per lead is when acquiring them. The cheaper the ad & the more conversions, the better performance (in most cases). Now take it further with attribution to see what the ROI was on your sales opportunities where those ads actually had an influence on closed-won opportunities and revenue. Now, you have a good foundation set up for ROI tracking with your PPC and online ad programs in Marketo!

Conclusion

I hope the knowledge shared in this book will help you and your team achieve your desired marketing result, without breaking your bank! The purpose of this book is to help teams expand on their knowledge when using Marketo, and to understand the best practices shared by consultants that charge and arm & a leg. I was one of them.

Use the tips, suggestions, and framework offered to build upon your operations and show your management team that you can get the job done without using marketing budget dollars, at least for what you learned in this book that is.

Here's to building better and more engaging Marketo programs!

Printed in Great Britain
by Amazon